From Boal to Jana Sanskriti

Jana Sanskriti is internationally recognised as the most iconic post-Boalian Theatre of the Oppressed operation in the world today.

This fully illustrated book by the Bengali company's founder and artistic director Sanjoy Ganguly, edited by Ralph Yarrow, collects and explains their programme of workshop exercises, placing them in the context of their social and activist work. A set of interviews with Ganguly complements these practical sequences, drawing in topics such as the role of the joker, the nature of development, participation and agency, aesthetics as transformation and Theatre of the Oppressed in the context of a market economy.

Sanjoy Ganguly is the founder and Artistic Director of the Jana Sanskriti Centre for the Theatre of the Oppressed, in West Bengal, India; considered by Boal the chief exponents of his methodology outside his native Brazil. He is the author of *Jana Sanskriti: Forum Theatre and Democracy in India* (Routledge, 2010).

Ralph Yarrow is Emeritus Professor of Drama and Comparative Literature at the University of East Anglia, UK.

Sanjoy Ganguly and Augusto Boal

From Boal to Jana Sanskriti
Practice and principles

Sanjoy Ganguly

Edited by
Ralph Yarrow

LONDON AND NEW YORK

First published 2017
by Routledge
2 Park Square, Milton Park, Abingdon, Oxon OX14 4RN

and by Routledge
605 Third Avenue, New York, NY 10017

First issued in paperback 2020

Routledge is an imprint of the Taylor & Francis Group, an informa business

© 2017 Sanjoy Ganguly; selection and editorial matter,
Ralph Yarrow

The right of the editor to be identified as the author of the editorial material, and of the author for his individual chapters, has been asserted in accordance with sections 77 and 78 of the Copyright, Designs and Patents Act 1988.

All rights reserved. No part of this book may be reprinted or reproduced or utilised in any form or by any electronic, mechanical, or other means, now known or hereafter invented, including photocopying and recording, or in any information storage or retrieval system, without permission in writing from the publishers.

Trademark notice: Product or corporate names may be trademarks or registered trademarks, and are used only for identification and explanation without intent to infringe.

British Library Cataloguing-in-Publication Data
A catalogue record for this book is available from the British Library

Library of Congress Cataloguing-in-Publication Data
A catalog record for this title has been requested

ISBN 13: 978-0-367-73689-7 (pbk)
ISBN 13: 978-1-138-22332-5 (hbk)

Typeset in Times New Roman
by Apex CoVantage, LLC

To Sima, Rohini, Satya, Pareshda,
Monoranjan da, Prashanta,
Renuka: the architects of Jana Sanskriti

And to

My younger brother, the main striker of my forward line,
Julian Boal

Contents

Foreword by Eugene van Erven   x
Preface by Ralph Yarrow   xiii
Notes on contributors   xvi

PART 1
Jana Sanskriti workshops   1
Developing Boal's games into social metaphors
SANJOY GANGULY

Introductory exercises   3
   While walking 3
   Feel the protagonist 5
   Express emotion 7
   Variation, finding oppression 8
   Indian parliament 9
   Fish society 10
   Game of power 13
   Expression with body 15

Jana Sanskriti workshops: Developing Boal's games into social metaphors   17
   Editor's introductory note 17

Workshop 1   19
   Exercise 1: Joint sculpture 19
   Exercise 2: Circles of emotion 22
   Exercise 3: Sculpting in pairs 25
   Variation of pair sculpting 27

viii *Contents*

Workshop 2 33
 Exercise 1: Human knot, plus variation 33
 Exercise 2: Variations of Grandmother's footsteps 41
  Variation 1: Deer and tiger 41
  Variation 2: Crossing the border 42
 Exercise 3: Spontaneous group sculptures 44
 Exercise 4: Development of status game 47

Workshop 3 53
 Exercise 1: Forum in a circle 53
 Exercise 2: Variation on Columbian hypnosis 56
  Variation 2: Columbian hypnosis 59
 Exercise 3: Blind game 62
 Exercise 4: Storytelling 64

Workshop 4 68
 Exercise 1: Catch in the circle 68
 Exercise 2: Newspaper theatre 69
 Exercise 3: Points of contact 71
 Exercise 4: Invisible friend 73
 Exercise 5: Soundscape and images 75
 Exercise 6: Characters' stories 78

Workshop 5 80
 Exercise 1: Moving as a still image 80
 Exercise 2: Experiencing the lives of others 80
 Exercise 3: Glass Cobra becomes the Trade Union Game 82

PART 2
Interviews with Sanjoy Ganguly and short essays 83
 Introductory note 83

Interview 1. Interview with Sima and Sanjoy Ganguly, November 2013 85
CONDUCTED BY ROBERT KLEMENT

 'About the rehearsal for total revolution and the
  practice of love' 86

Interview 2. Interview with Sanjoy Ganguly, 30 July 2013   91
CONDUCTED BY ROBYN KIRKBY

**Interview 3. Interview with Sanjoy Ganguly,
27 December 2013**   106
CONDUCTED BY CLÉMENT POUTOT

**Interview 4. Interview with Sanjoy Ganguly,
November 2014, Vienna**   118
CONDUCTED BY JOSCHKA KÖCK

**Interview 5. Interview with Sanjoy Ganguly,
on Vivekananda, January 2014**   122
CONDUCTED BY CLÉMENT POUTOT

**The political aesthetic of Jana Sanskriti: Theatre as an art
of creating connection**   133
SANJOY GANGULY

Coda: 'Aesthetics as transformation'   141
SANJOY GANGULY

**Postscript: A critical space: Forum, jokering and the
problem of sympathy**   144
SANJOY GANGULY

**Letters from Augusto Boal and Sanjoy Ganguly,
March/April 2009**   148

Bibliography   153

Foreword

It is an unseasonably cold spring morning in Holland in the middle of April 2016. Here, in northwestern Europe, we live in unsettling times. Tens of thousands of refugees from Syria, Somalia, Eritrea and beyond are flooding into our communities, while countless of their fellows continue to perish during perilous migrations across the Mediterranean. Less than a month ago and just two hours south by train from where I write this, Islamic State–affiliated terrorists created a bloodbath in Brussels. Commuting to work, entering city centres, returning home to our dwellings to eat and sleep: none of this is self-evident any longer for the relatively well-off in the West. As if it ever were.

I have just reread the five interviews with Sanjoy Ganguly at the end of this collection of texts about Jana Sanskriti. I am struck once again by the clarity of analysis in them, the provocative critical thinking, the worldwide applicability of ideas that have been evolving collectively over more than thirty years from local roots firmly planted in the soil and culture of rural West Bengal. The journey of Jana Sanskriti is part of a much larger story about engaged, participatory community-based art that has been spreading across the globe after World War II. Importantly, it is not a story that originated in the North, but one that in the 1970s and 80s was at the very least significantly propelled by artists in Brazil, India and other places in the South. In a serendipitous way it also intersects with my own involvement in what is arguably the most relevant (and extensive) arts movement today.

In May 1985, more or less around the time that Jana Sanskriti was born, I completed a book-length study of popular political theatre companies in the West. Some of these groups are still around today and have acquired legendary status. Like Jana Sanskriti, many of them were interested in regional traditions and folk culture, employing their idiom to emancipate urban and rural working-class audiences. But unlike Jana Sanskriti, they were more about communicating a ready-made political message than actively involving their audiences in its construction. In January 1986, I arrived in Mumbai, India. It was the first leg of an ethnographic research trip through the political theatre landscape of Asia that would last until May 1988. I didn't meet Sanjoy Ganguly and his group, although I came geographically to within a few kilometers when I interviewed and studied the work of playwrights like Utpal Dutt and Badal Sircar in Kolkata. It was a near miss, because more than these nationally recognised political artists I was actually looking for grassroots activists like Sanjoy. Further along in my journey, I would meet some of these in Delhi, Kerala and Orissa – and in February and March 1986 in the middle of a civil war in the Philippines. But that is a different story: one that also contains elements of Boal, Freire and the ambition to generate a nationwide humanist arts movement nourished from the grassroots.

I finally did meet Sanjoy and other members of Jana Sanskriti in June 2008, when they visited my country on the invitation of Formaat, the only professional Theatre of the Oppressed company in the Netherlands. Like the International Community Arts Festival (ICAF) that I direct, Formaat is based in the city of Rotterdam, one of the largest and busiest ports in the world. I am sure that location and its function as a global transport hub has something to do with both ICAF's and Formaat's desire to foster worldwide connections and cross-fertilisation. Not coincidentally, Rotterdam is also one of the most culturally diverse places in Europe, including a large diasporic Indian community (descendants of indented labourers who, after the trans-Atlantic slave trade was abolished, went to Surinam and the Netherlands Antilles). It made Jana Sanskriti's street performance of *Golden Girl* less of an exoticizing experience than it might have been in other places. Much the same could be said of the day-long workshop Sanjoy had facilitated a few days earlier for a group of young Dutch community artists.

While I merely intuited the sophisticated cross-cultural quality of Jana Sanskriti's aesthetics and techniques during this first encounter in 2008, I learned to rationally and affectively appreciate it more while actively participating in Sanjoy's version of Boal's Glass Cobra game in December 2015. This time, the occasion was an international Theatre of the Oppressed festival organised by Formaat. Until then, I had understood this exercise to be a relatively quick and effective get-to-know-you exercise in Boal's arsenal of games for activating the senses. In Sanjoy's hands and with a truly intercontinental group of participants, however, the game turned into an extended analytic exploration of relations in the workplace that lasted close to three hours. It is that thoroughness, that refusal to be rushed, that gentle insistence to dig ever deeper and continuously investigate new angles that characterises Jana Sanskriti's approach and makes it work across borders. The interviews at the end of this volume further reveal why and how.

They emphasise the importance of reciprocal, egalitarian and long-lasting relationships between artist-activists and what Sanjoy – with an obvious wink to Boal – calls 'spect-activists'. In the case of Jana Sanskriti these relationships evolve over several generations and across multiple racial, social, political, cultural and gender boundaries. They also involve direct action well beyond the theatre space, including social organizing and progressive entrepreneurship. While reflecting on these extraordinary relational dynamics and activities, Sanjoy addresses a wide range of pertinent themes, for both India and the world at large. They include a critique of patriarchy, postcolonial and party politics (both of the socialist and capitalist variety), as well as market-driven economies and industrial agriculture. However, he also does not shy away from occasional criticism of overly dogmatic and opportunistic practitioners of Theatre of the Oppressed. Perhaps most significantly, rather than quick fixes for social problems or vehicles for ideological manipulation, Sanjoy regards his workshops and Forum performances as genuinely collective processes that generate critical thinking that is never finished. It is crucial to the development of thoughtful, responsible citizens, regardless of their background or whether they live in rural West Bengal or urban Rotterdam. The totality of that work, which extends over time and across the globe, constitutes the unique art of Jana Sanskriti.

It is dialogical aesthetics in the truest sense of the term.

Eugene van Erven

Preface

Jana Sanskriti is the leading exponent of Theatre of the Oppressed (TO) in India, working largely with rural populations in West Bengal from its base just to the north of Kolkata. It has operated since 1985 and, in addition to coordinating and supporting more than thirty performance teams in West Bengal, reaching thousands of people every year, has established the Indian Federation of Theatre of the Oppressed to create links with activist groups in many other states in India and assist them to learn and practise TO. It was recognised by Augusto Boal as a leading world example of the sustained and successful practice of Theatre of the Oppressed, the method of activist theatre he spent his life developing (see Boal, *Theatre of the Oppressed, Games for Actors and Non-Actors, The Rainbow of Desire, Legislative Theatre, Aesthetics of the Oppressed*). In what follows, the first steps to the embodied acquisition of that power of agency are clearly laid out.

In Part 1, this book contains detailed illustrated workshop sequences compiled by Sanjoy Ganguly, artistic director of Jana Sanskriti (for an account of their work during the first twenty-five years of their operation, see Ganguly, *Jana Sanskriti: Forum Theatre and Democracy in India*, Routledge 2010). Part 2 consists of extracts from interviews and discussions with Ganguly in which he explains how and why these sequences represent key aspects of Jana Sanskriti's development of theatre activists and the practice they engage in, followed by some short essays in which he discusses guiding principles of the work, and an exchange of mails between Ganguly and Boal which signals the closeness of their relationship.

Ganguly retains Boal's terminology of the 'oppressed'. There has been extensive discussion in the TO movement and in work about it and other kinds of 'applied', interventionist, community' or 'development' theatre; some practitioners have come up with alternatives. In India and in the immediate context of Jana Sanskriti's work, it is clear that external forms of political and economic oppression are still widespread; of course, the groups they affect may also be designated as marginalised or disadvantaged in a variety of ways. Oppression, however, as Boal recognised, is also a state of mind and needs to be addressed both individually and internally, as well as collectively. The term recognises a significant distinction between being a victim and being able to take action. Ganguly further emphasises the essential distinction between 'theatre of' and 'theatre for' the oppressed, and sees his work as a way towards both internal and external revolution.

The workshop sequences draw on games and exercises by Boal and others and are used by Jana Sanskriti in training and rehearsal. In practice, Ganguly varies and adapts them depending on time and circumstance, and above all with the needs of the group he is working with in mind. What is important in using them is to bear this in mind and to listen to and observe the group. As Ganguly often says, the facilitator depends on the group rather than the other way around. The exercises should not be applied and prescribed as a set of 'techniques' or master-classes, but related to the needs and goals of the participants. Attitude is more important than accuracy.

The exercises are organised into six sections. How they are used can of course be altered to suit circumstances, but it is also important to note that only a small number of exercises are given under each section: that is because each one is explored in depth, working intensively on each stage, and quite often involves a number of variations as well. Sanjoy Ganguly often spends between one and two hours on each exercise, sometimes more. If done in this way they enable participants to explore many of the key transactions which take place in the creation of a Forum piece, and the kinds of interaction with other performers and potentially with spectators which may be required. They also enable the performers to observe and interrogate their own work, to 'be the spectator of their own action', which is an essential skill in both Forum performance and the subsequent analysis of its operation and implications for action beyond the stage.

Each section can be seen as a self-contained sequence (or as an example of a sequence in which individual components can be replaced or adapted to suit particular geographical, political or social circumstances): there is generally an increasing degree of complexity as participants are taken through stages of interacting together, of collective creation and of collaborative reflection about the situations and responses which they are recognising and expressing.

For example, the workshops often progress from constructing individual images to pairs of images and/or group images (participants use their bodies to show an image and then link up with/respond to others), then analysing what kinds of situation these depict and naming them; they move onto a variety of methods to dynamise (activate) these images and begin to develop text related to them – for example, by asking participants making images to come up with nonverbal sounds or gibberish, then with single words, then with a complete sentence and perhaps with an 'inner monologue' which articulates their feelings in the moment. After some time scenes begin to emerge and other phases – crisis points, key moments of conflict, justifications and defences – begin to emerge and can eventually be written down and later edited so that a composite performance script is produced which emerges directly from the participants' experience.

Underlying this work, Ganguly's key principles are that these games and exercises are part of a theatrical and political aesthetic (which he explains in essays at the end of the volume): a development of bodily, emotional and intellectual awareness which enables individuals to join together to create social metaphors of their world and the structures of power which shape it, so that these structures may be open to question and revision. The exercises enable participants to engage in the move from particular to general, from concrete to abstract, which means that the scenarios they create have both visceral and direct as well as symbolic and collective impact. Ganguly's previous book (Routledge 2010) demonstrates precisely how this plays out in the Indian political scene and in the daily lives of the many thousands Jana Sanskriti's work has affected over the last thirty years.

The trajectory towards what he calls 'scripting [the] play', rather than 'playing [the] script' (Ganguly 2010: 99, 128–9) emerges during all these sequences. It is the key to Jana Sanskriti's ethic and philosophy of relationship and collective action, which transfers the means of production, as Boal desired, to those whose acquisition of voice and agency can most tellingly allow them henceforth to script their own world.

Ralph Yarrow

Notes on contributors

Sanjoy Ganguly was active in Communist politics as a student. Disillusioned by its centralist tendencies, he left the party to search for a political culture of dialogue and democracy. He began working in the theatre in rural Bengal in the early 1980s. His encounter several years later with Augusto Boal and the Theatre of the Oppressed, coupled with his own passionate commitment to the creation of a more just and equal society, led him to found Jana Sanskriti, an independent organisation committed to the use of theatre to conscientise and empower the communities it serves. With more than thirty active theatre groups associated with the group, Jana Sanskriti is now the largest organisation of its kind in India.

Robyn Kirkby is a drama teacher who has spent eight years working at inner city schools in the UK. Robyn first encountered TO while training with Chris Vine at City University New York and later with Cardboard Citizens in London. TO's principles have been central to her teaching practice ever since and she has delivered international workshops on using forum theatre in schools. Robyn visited Jana Sanskriti in 2013 and 2014 while researching her paper *Fighting Patriarchy from the Grassroots: A Case Study of Jana Sanskriti*. She is based in Bristol but is about to embark on a two-year adventure teaching drama in Bogotá, Colombia.

Robert Klement has worked and lived as a Theatre of the Oppressed practitioner in Germany, Italy and Austria. He studied dramatherapy and engages himself in working with personal and collective stories of migration and neighbourhood/community transformation.

Joschka Köck is a TO practitioner at Theater der Unterdrückten Wien and an MA student of Development Studies at the University of Vienna. His bachelor thesis was a case study of Jana Sanskriti and how it is producing emancipatory collective knowledge through forum theatre.

Clément Poutot is currently a lecturer in the Department of Sociology and Anthropology at the University of Caen, Normandy, France. His PhD focused on the practice of TO. Using an historical and comparative approach, his thesis, entitled *Le théâtre de l'opprimé, matrice symbolique de l'espace public* (The Theatre of the Oppressed: A Symbolic Matrix of Public Spaces), presents a study of three processes in different locations: the creation process in Latin America through the experience of Augusto Boal; in France through various Theatre of the Oppressed groups; and in West Bengal, India, around the teams and committees that constitute the Jana Sanskriti movement.

Eugene van Erven is Professor of Media, Performance and the City at Utrecht University, Netherlands, where he has taught literature, drama and community arts courses. He also works 'on loan' as artistic director of the International Community Arts Festival in Rotterdam (www.icafrotterdam.com). Part of his task is to stimulate academic discourse on participation in the arts and to foster sustainable partnerships between Media and Culture Studies and professionals in the culture and media sector. His most important books are: *Radical People's Theatre* (Indiana University Press, 1988), *The Playful Revolution: Theatre and Liberation in Asia* (Indiana 1992) and *Community Theatre: Global Perspectives* (Routledge 2001). His most recent works include *Community Art Power: Essays from ICAF 2011* (RWT, 2013) and *Community Arts Dialogues* (Treaty of Utrecht, 2013).

Ralph Yarrow is Emeritus Professor of Drama and Comparative Literature at the University of East Anglia, Norwich, UK. He is a teacher, theatre director, performer, actor trainer, writer, editor, translator and project leader. His key areas of work are: Transcultural Theatre; Applied Theatre Practice; Theatre as/and Pedagogy. He has published books on Improvisation; Indian Theatre; European Theatre; Sacred Theatre; and many articles and chapters in books. Recent writing is about links between performance practice and process and i) Ecology; ii) Democracy and Politics; iii) Indian performance theory. He has worked closely with Jana Sanskriti since 1999.

Part 1
Jana Sanskriti Workshops
Developing Boal's games into social metaphors

Sanjoy Ganguly

Introductory exercises

While walking

First step: The participating actors will first form a circle.

Second step: With the clap of the joker, the actors move around the circular space in multiple directions, taking up the whole circular space.

Third step: With the next clap of the joker, the actors freeze wherever they are in the circle. Now the joker asks all the actors to choose an animal or a bird and represent them using their bodies.

Fourth step: Now the actors move in the circle imitating the animals and birds they have chosen for themselves.

Fifth step: Now the actors roaming in the circle will come closer and make pairs. The actors in these pairs will exchange their images. That means actor 'A' will take the image of 'B' and actor 'B' will take the image of 'A'. Now this process of give and take will continue until each actor has covered all the other actors. The time for the exchange of image between two actors each time should not take more than a few seconds.

Sixth step: Now the actors move in the circle as the last image they received; the actors each look for the image which they made at the beginning of the exercise. After locating their original image, the actors each will hand over the image they are currently embodying to the person in whom they find their own image and then stand at the circumference of the circular space. The rest of the actors continue the exercise until each has found his/her original image.

Feel the protagonist

Actors get divided into groups. Each group will have three to four actors.

Each group will make an image of oppression where the conflict between oppressor and oppressed characters is clear and concrete. Each group will be identified by a number given by the facilitator, like group number 1, 2, 3, 4.

Now group No 1 and group No 3 will stand face to face. Each of them will observe the image of each other. For example, group No 3 will observe the image of group No 1 and vice-versa.

Now the observer group will express their feeling about the protagonist portrayed by the other group through images while the image of oppression will be maintained by the actors of the other group. Each actor will show his/her own image about the protagonist.

Now at this stage the observer group will make an image of oppression which will be seen by the other group.

A similar process will have to be done by the group which observed the image; they have to now portray the feelings about the protagonist they have observed while the performers hold their image.

The two groups will keep playing this game until the facilitator asks them to stop. One group will make an image of an oppression and the other group will express their feeling about the protagonist, then the roles will be reversed. The feeling expressed about the protagonist can be concrete or abstract, it can reflect the will or desire of the protagonist, or it can be simply a reproduction of the image of the oppressed.

Express emotion

The actors will make two lines facing each other. On the clap of the facilitator they will turn around so that they face away from each other. There will be an equal number of actors in each line. Every actor will choose the actor in front of him/her as a partner to whom s/he will communicate. The actors of both lines will be given different emotions – for example, one group can be given the emotion of love and the other can be given the emotion of anger to express with a dynamised, moving image.

Now the actors turn around and each one of them faces the actor standing opposite to him/her. Two actors standing face to face will play the game together. The facilitator gives different emotions to each group. Suppose the facilitator would ask actors of one group to play the emotion of anger and the other group the emotion of love.

Now with the clap of the facilitator, one actor from each group comes slowly closer with the emotion given by the facilitator; they exchange the emotion in the middle of their journey and continue to move following the same direction away from each other to join the opposite line of actors. The actors thus change their position. The facilitator asks two actors from each line to do the same until everyone completes their turn.

Variation, finding oppression

Now each actor in one line will play an oppressor character. He/she has to improvise the character. The characters will have to be real and not imaginary. The actors of the other group will play the oppressed character; they also have to improvise a real oppressed character that they often see around them and experience often too. With the clap of the facilitator, one oppressor and one oppressed character from each group come closer.

Initially they interact nonverbally and then the facilitator asks them to speak; the actors improvise the text. Now the facilitator at some point stops the interaction, and the actors playing oppressor and oppressed hold the image when the facilitator claps.

In the next step the facilitator asks other actors standing in both groups to come and replace the protagonist and play the character; actors keep coming, replace the oppressed character and act for a minute each time – like a 'lightning Forum'. This is how actors can discuss their reality and find stories for scripting Forum plays. After one story is played for a few minutes, another two actors from each group depict an oppression and involve others in discussing that.

Indian parliament

The actors will make two lines facing each other. With the clap of the facilitator they will turn around. There will be an equal number of actors in each line. Every actor will choose the actor opposite him/her as a partner to whom s/he will communicate. The actors of one group will represent members of the government bench and the others will represent members of the opposition.

Now in this step one actor from the government and one actor from the opposition come and make an image of themselves in the house. Others will observe in a semi-circle. On the call of the facilitator the actors will speak to each other.

Now the leader of the opposition or the ruling party will be replaced by other actors. After one episode of argument one actor from each group will create another scene of the parliament.

10 *Sanjoy Ganguly*

Fish society

The actors will walk randomly in a circular movement like fishes in an aquarium. The facilitator will walk along with the actors with a ball in hand. The ball is considered to be food for the fishes.

Introductory exercises 11

Now the facilitator asks the actors playing fishes to come very close to each other. The facilitator places the ball between the mouths of two actors. Each actor has to use his/her hands as the fins of the fish. The actors cannot hold the ball with their hands.

Everyone will try to reach the food. But no one will be able to reach it. The fishes will keep moving until they are asked to stop.

Now actors will each be requested to represent their experience through a word which is to be written on a flip chart. After everyone writes, the facilitator will divide the actors into groups. There will be five to six actors in each group. Each group will examine and discuss all the words written on the chart. They will then choose one of the words and make an image of that word. When one group presents their image, the others observe.

1.

2.

Game of power

Actors will make a circle. They will be asked to think about the power relations in the society we live in. They have to divide the society into seven different tiers or layers. The facilitator will randomly give a number to each actor, between 1 and 7; any number can be given to any actor. Actors having the number will have to think of portraying a character that falls under the number given. Higher numbers will indicate more powerful characters we see in the society, lower numbers will indicate less powerful. Actors given 1 and 2 will be the powerless section of the society in a way. After explaining and giving a number to everyone, the facilitator will ask the actors to turn around and sketch the characters in mind they have to depict.

After a while the facilitator asks if the actors have found their characters. If actors raise their hands, it will mean they are ready.

Now the actors come to the arena acting out the character nonverbally. All of them will keep portraying their characters, they interact with some invisible characters to clearly depict the characters. For example, a teacher character can act inside his classroom where there is no student visible. The characters will each relate to their invisible character, they won't relate to other actors unless the facilitator asks them.

In this step, actors will speak to their imaginary invisible characters in their own mother tongue. For example, an actor with number 1 is an agricultural labourer, so s/he would speak to his/her boss, who may be a middle farmer.

Now the facilitator asks actors to relate to other actors present in the arena with their characters. Since there will be seven different classes of people, there will be even and uneven interactions continuing for some time among the characters portrayed by the actors. If two number 7's speak to each other, that will be one kind of dialogue; when there is a conversation between numbers 1 and 6, numbers 2 and 5, numbers 3 and 4, numbers 4 and 6 etc., actors will keep having different kinds of experience. Each actor has to interact with all other actors. No interaction will continue for more than two minutes.

Introductory exercises 15

This is how the exercise will continue until everyone completes an interaction with all others. The facilitator will ask everyone to relax and then will divide the actors into groups of five to six people. The group should be divided in a way so that each group can have characters of all strata of the society. The group will work together to produce an image of power in the society. One by one the group will present their images of power.

Expression with body

Here an actor from the participants wears a mask having no expression. S/he will be given a character and a theme which s/he has to act. Suppose the actor with a mask on his face (the face can be covered with a piece of cloth) is a worker trying to enter his owner's residence. The actor now has to portray all the inhibitions, anxiety, anger, doubts, anticipation etc. with his face covered either by an expressionless mask or by a cloth.

After some time, another actor comes in: s/he can be an ally of the first character or an antagonist. Based on the theme given by the facilitator, they act and create a story. The whole exercise will be like miming. No words will be used. The whole body of both actors except their faces will speak and make the story very clear to the observer participants.

Jana Sanskriti workshops
Developing Boal's games into social metaphors

Editor's introductory note

These illustrated examples of workshop practice show sequences of games and exercises used by Jana Sanskriti in training its actor-activists and in scripting the plays which they construct in order to articulate and interrogate their real-life experience.

The exercises draw on the underlying principles of Augusto Boal's work, which aim to develop the capacity of the body to register and articulate experience through the senses, to investigate its social and political dynamics through reflection and analysis and to train the ability to use these processes to collectively create interactive and interrogative dramaturgies.

The illustrations show the Jana Sanskriti core team working at their Centre in Badu. In many cases the exercises require the participants to create images and the initial stages of scenarios, and it is clear that these are derived from the personal experience of the performers.

Many people have remarked on the extraordinary expressivity of Jana Sanskriti's actors. None of them had conventional theatre training; they have followed the kinds of work illustrated here. Of course there are some cultural factors – their performances draw on elements of Indian folk style like dance and song and comic repartee, and Ganguly has pointed to the capacity of folk forms to take an irreverent and ironic stance to icons and authority figures. These elements, together with a richness of colour, spectacle and rhythm – albeit produced with very simple materials – are used to assist communication and underpin the political strategy of the work to engage and to challenge. Thus also the fact that their work is a 'fusion' of Indian and 'Western' modes is a way of incorporating this dialogic and interrogative dynamic. It is why their work is both essentially Indian and radically international.

The accompanying text gives many indications of the aims and outcomes of these exercises. However, neither these nor the sequences in which they appear are hard and fast. Sanjoy Ganguly says: 'I don't think a sequence is necessary. A facilitator should decide when an exercise will be appropriate and in which context. I have no faith in fixed modules. These exercises are to establish the fact that we need to improvise based on our political need and our perspective of Theatre of the Oppressed or other forms of theatre. The exercises in the book are expected to be improvised further by practitioners according to the political context they work with.'

Workshop 1

Exercise 1: Joint sculpture

1. The group starts by standing in a circle. The facilitator claps his/her hands and the participants start moving around the circle. The group should try and fill all the gaps in order to balance the space.

2. On the facilitator's second clap, the group should freeze. The group should check to see if there are any gaps. If the participants are unable to balance the space, keep repeating until they are able to achieve this.

3. The facilitator tells the participants that they are going to catch a train, in order to give the participants a purpose whilst moving around the space. The facilitator should then increase the tempo after each clap by telling the group that there are five minutes until the train, followed by three, two and then one minute, finally the whistle is blown at the end of the activity. The performers are reminded throughout the activity that they are not able to run.
4. The group goes back to the speed when the train is five minutes away, this time when the facilitator claps his/her hands, the group should join hands with two other group members. The joining of hands should cause a change in muscle tension, as the participants should have to stretch their bodies in order to reach each other: no straight lines are allowed. This part of the exercise should be developed into an abstract image. At this point the warm-up exercise has developed into collectively developing an abstract sculpture. The group should incorporate different levels and layers with their bodies.

5. In order to move from the abstract into concrete reality, half of the group become spectators whilst the other half repeat the activity, walking

Workshop 1 21

around the space, then creating a group sculpture on the facilitator's clap. The group should aim to make the image as beautiful as possible using their bodies.

6. The facilitator asks the group to slowly disconnect and stand up straight, then he or she claps and the participants return to the group sculpture. The facilitator questions the spectators as to which image is more aesthetically pleasing. (Most groups prefer the connected group image, whilst a few prefer the disconnected image, but it is good to give the group the choice.)

7. The spectators are then asked to name the image using their own experiences to interpret the abstract to clearly ground it in their own reality. Example titles from our workshop include, 'Determination', 'Connection' and 'Surprise'. The group should repeat this exercise three times whilst the spectators are encouraged to move around the image and observe it from multiple angles in order to gain multiple perspectives. The third time, the spectators are asked to create a concrete story from the image; this allows the spectator to think outside the rehearsal room into reality.

22 Sanjoy Ganguly

8. The spectators should now swap over so that all participants are able to both perform and observe the images. It is also possible to think of concrete stories from the images of disconnection.

Exercise 2: Circles of emotion

1. This activity requires six circles to be drawn on the floor with chalk. The six circles should make one large circle. Inside each circle an emotion is written – for example: aggression, pity, jealousy, calmness, frustration or anger.
2. Participants should stand in a circle over the chalk circles so that they are facing in the same direction. When the facilitator claps his/her hands, the group should move in a circle like a rotating wheel.

3. When the facilitator claps his/her hands a second time, the participants should stop. They should then create an image that represents the emotion that is in the circle they are standing in. They should remember a time when they personally felt that emotion in order to ground it in reality. The emotion should be shown throughout the whole body, not just the face. This should be repeated a few more times in order for the participants to explore a range of emotions.

Workshop 1 23

4. The second stage of this activity requires the actors to choose a concrete story behind the emotions they are going to portray. The performers are given a small amount of time to consider their story to make sure that their story is clear.

5. A member of the group can then choose a few participants and sculpt an image in order to create a story. Those not involved in the group image come out to observe and interpret the image. The facilitator should question the spectators in order to find out what they see in the image and to give the image a title. The group should use their own experiences to explain the story shown in the image so that various dimensions of reality are exposed. This allows the participants to gain an understanding of their own and others' realities. This stage can be repeated multiple times in order to explore a range of images so that the group can choose one to be the focus.

6. Using one of the images that have been shared, the group should explore the image in smaller groups in order to create three images based on the original. Our troupe, in groups of five, chose a story of domestic violence.
7. Finally, each group should share their three images with the rest of the participants. Through experiencing the different interpretations of the story, the group are able to see a broader picture and consider different dimensions of one situation.

Exercise 3: Sculpting in pairs

1. The participants are put into pairs; one will become an artist and the other will become the clay from which he/she is to be sculpted. The

artists move their partners into an image of their choice. When they are finished, they should stand to the side to observe their creations.

2. Within the pairs, the participants should swap roles and repeat the activity.
3. All participants should then stand together on stage in their sculpted form. One member of the group then chooses several sculptures in order

to create a group image. The rest of the group observes the image and chooses a concrete story to describe it; symbolism should not be used, as the image should be firmly grounded in reality.

4. The participants in the group image should then become the spectators, the rest of the group should go back on stage and create their sculptures so that a different participant can make a new group image with new group members. Again, those that are not in the image should observe and create a concrete story and title for the image.
5. This should be repeated so that all of the sculptures have been used. In a large group of forty-five participants, around seven or eight stories could be told.

Variation of pair sculpting

1. In pairs, the artists create a sculpture of a person they know very well who is being oppressed: they should not create an image of themselves. They should also have a detailed knowledge of the oppressor; this activity should be completed in silence. In this variation of the game, men can play women and vice-versa. The artists come together and observe their creations.

2. The artists then return to the stage and pose as the oppressors themselves in order to create a clear image of oppression.

Workshop 1   29

3. Within the pairs, the actors should bring the story to life without words on the facilitator's clap. The performance should continue to be improvised until the facilitator claps again, at which point they should freeze.

4. The group should make an audience. The facilitator will ask for a pair to enter the performance space to share their silent performance. The pair will create their image onstage. On the facilitator's first clap the pair should come alive in their mimed performance. On the second clap they should both use the words 'ooh la la' instead of normal speech. When the facilitator thinks the spectators have seen enough, he/she should clap a third time so that the pair will freeze in a strong image.
5. The audience should be questioned by the facilitator in order to create a concrete story of what is going on. The facilitator should deepen their story by asking questions which will develop their idea, such as: 'what are their names?'; 'is he/she employed?'; 'where is the scene set?' The facilitator should encourage as many details as possible in order to help the performers and make the story clearly grounded in reality. After hearing three or four suggestions, the facilitator should choose one suggestion for the performers to play out in a role-play. The pair should improvise the suggested story using real words. The performers will tell the story that is given by the spectators.
6. This is repeated, with every pair starting from their own frozen image. It is also possible for the pair to choose their own story so that they start improvising with real words straight after the 'ooh la la' stage, without asking the audience.

Workshop 1   31

Please note that the protagonists should not always be portrayed as a simple victim, instead they can be played as someone trying to change their situation, as this gives hope to the spectators and encourages intervention and ideas.

Here are examples of stories explored in our workshop:

- A mistress being punished by her illegitimate lover, as he believed she was having an affair.

- A man trafficking a young girl who pleads to be able to return home.

Note: These exercises start from a similar model to that used by Boal, *Games for Actors and Non-Actors,* 1992 in the sequence on pp. 127ff. in that book. They also employ a similar technique of 'dynamisation' to that which Boal introduces. But as always with Ganguly's work they are extended explicitly and sequentially towards the engagement with specific experiences and circumstances from the world of the participants and they move over an extended period of time towards the creation of quite developed scenarios. Each exercise may last well in excess of an hour, sometimes up to a whole day depending on the time-frame available. (Ed.)

Workshop 2

Exercise 1: Human knot

1. The group joins hands in a circle. Throughout the activity the participants should keep their hands joined.

2. One person, usually the facilitator, is making/leading the knot. The group should tangle themselves by going under people's arms and stepping over people's arms in order to create a human knot. The facilitator should guide the group so that by the end they are completely tangled, with little space between each participant. The facilitator steps out of the knot.

3. They should now untangle themselves without letting go of each other's hands. By the end of the activity, the group should be standing back in a circle.

Note: This is similar to Boal's 'The Circle of Knots' (*Games* . . ., 67–8)

Variation of human knot

1. The group should use circular movements so that they are weaving around each other within a very small space.

2. The facilitator claps to freeze the group. Whilst still, each group member should join hands with two other group members, making sure that their right hand is joined to another person's left hand and that their left hand is joined to another person's right hand. This should be completed with very little speaking to help with concentration and focus.

36 *Sanjoy Ganguly*

3. When the group are all joined together, the participants should close their eyes and imagine that they are trapped in this position, like a lion in a net. Whilst keeping their eyes closed, the group should attempt to untangle themselves, keeping silent throughout the activity. It is important that the facilitator keeps a close eye on the group to make sure they are safe and do not hurt themselves whilst their eyes are closed.

4. After a while of trying to untangle themselves, the group should freeze on the facilitator's clap and reflect on how they are feeling in that situation. The group should then open their eyes and remaining silent, continue to try and untangle the knot.
5. On the facilitator's clap, the group should close their eyes again for a moment and return to the circle. Participants should face out from the circle with their eyes closed in order to collect the feelings they experienced throughout the activity. They should then communicate this feeling through an individual image.

6. When the individual group members are ready, they should face inwards and share their images.

7. The participants should observe the other images in the circle and move towards people whom they feel have chosen a similar feeling to themselves.
8. When the participants have separated into several groups, each representing a different feeling, the facilitator should number each group. The actors make an audience. One by one, the groups come to the stage and the members each freeze in the individual image they created. On the facilitator's clap, the participants on stage add movement to their image, without moving their feet.

9. On the next clap, the participants should say out loud the feeling they have chosen and repeat the word or phrase as they portray their moving image. After they have shared with the group, the participants should write their word or phrase on a flipchart for the group to see. Examples of responses in our group: two wrote "impossible", two wrote "complex", five wrote "we must do it", two wrote "keep patient". It can be seen that the participants responded with varying levels of hope and resistance.
10. The participants are then put into smaller groups of five or six, and in their groups will choose a word or phrase from the flipchart. From this, they should create one still image that portrays oppression. Their image should have a concrete story behind it, with a clear idea of the characters and the power relations between them.
11. After some time, the groups share their image with the group, one by one. The facilitator asks the audience to interpret each image. Examples in our

group were a man attempting to escape the consumerist concerns of his family, who crave consumer goods while others cannot afford medicine; three men drinking alcohol and harassing young girls, displaying patriarchal values; and a girl being sexually harassed by her school teacher.

12. The groups should then develop their still image into a sequence of three still images in order to show their story in more detail. Each group should then show the story to the rest of the participants. During each sequence, an audience member, chosen by the facilitator, should narrate the sequence in detail, giving names to the characters and explaining the relationships clearly. This should be a continuous commentary of the three still images: the facilitator should not allow the audience member to stop describing at any point so that the commentary is made to be as detailed as possible. A story our group created was of a girl going to school who is sexually harassed by her teacher. When she tells her parents, they do not believe her and punish her for being outspoken. The next day at school, when the teacher harasses her, she defends herself and shouts at him. Her classmates do not react and so passively support the teacher in his oppression.

Through broadening the purpose of this game from a physical warm-up to an ensemble building activity, the group is allowed to develop stories that explore and criticise their own reality.

Exercise 2: Variations of Grandmother's footsteps

Variation 1: Deer and tiger

1. One group member, representing a fascist tiger, stands on one side of the rehearsal space with his or her back to the rest of the group, who are at the other end of the rehearsal space. They represent the deer in the woods.

42 Sanjoy Ganguly

2. The object of the game is for the deer to kill the fascist tiger by touching him or her without the tiger seeing them. The deer should be ready to sacrifice their lives in order for one deer to be able to defeat the tiger so that there can be democracy in the wood.
3. The tiger can look back at any time without warning, as they are in constant fear of being killed. If the tiger sees a deer moving towards him, they are instantly killed and are out of the game. The game finishes when the tiger is killed.

Variation 2: Crossing the border

1. The tiger figure now represents border control police, who again stand on the other side of the rehearsal space with their back to the group. The group is divided into subgroups of three representing families trying to cross the border. They must stay together at all times in one clear group. We used the example of trying to cross the border from Morocco into Spain.
2. Again the police can turn round at any time. If the police see any person moving, his or her entire group will all be out of the game.

3. If at any point the facilitator sees an interesting frozen image, created by a particular family, s/he can pause the game so that the rest of the group are able to analyse and explore the meaning in the image and create an interpretation grounded in reality. An example of an interpretation made by Jana Sanskriti is a mother trying to escape from a violent family member with her children without being caught.

44 *Sanjoy Ganguly*

Exercise 3: Spontaneous group sculptures

1. Within the circle, the participants are divided into groups of four, who need to stand in a staggered arrangement rather than a straight line. The facilitator numbers the group members within each group, beginning with group 1.

2. A rhythm is played on a drum. When the final beat is played, all actors assume a still image of their choice.
3. When the rhythm begins again, the participants who were given the number 1 move counter-clockwise to join the next group. They will observe the image and assume their own still image that they feel adds to the image to create meaning.

4. The next time the rhythm starts, the participants given the number 2 will rotate counter-clockwise to the next group and assume a frozen image that again brings meaning to the image.
5. This stage will be repeated so that each group member has rotated to a new group and a completely new image is formed.

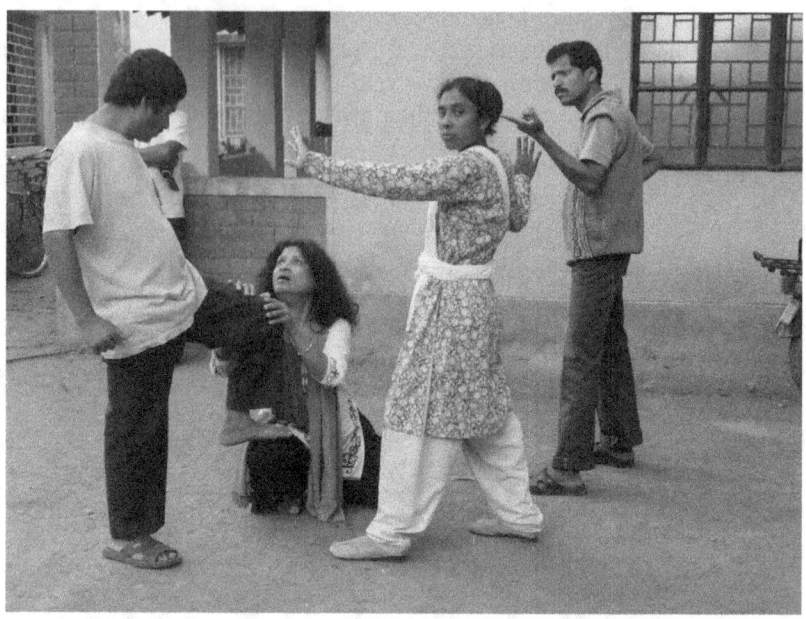

6. On the final round, the facilitator instructs the participants to remember their images. Each group shares their image, one by one, whilst the rest of the group explore the various meanings within each image.

Examples of images made by our groups are:

- A husband beating his wife while the mother-in-law and neighbour intervene.
- Villagers discovering the body of a man murdered for political reasons.
- A husband exiling his wife while her sisters attempt to console her.

Exercise 4: Development of status game

1. Everyone in the group stands in a circle and is given a number between 1 and 8. Each number relates to a specific status in society:

    8 = power, 7 = close to power, 6 = rich, 5 = upper middle class, 4 = middle class, 3 = just enough money to support their family, 2 = living day to day on whatever money they can earn, 1 = barely able to survive, as they have next to nothing.

2. The group are asked to turn around to face the outside of the circle in order to consider the character they will portray based on the number

they are given. In their own time, they should turn back to the centre of the circle when they have formulated an idea for their character.
3. The facilitator chooses an actor to enter the circle who begins miming his/her character in the centre of the circle. One by one, the rest of the characters are added.

4. When the whole group are all acting, the facilitator will clap his/her hands in order for the group to freeze. The performers are now allowed to communicate only using 'ooh la la' in place of real words.

5. On the second clap, the actors freeze again and are instructed by the facilitator to search for and interact with people of their own class, still only using the words 'ooh la la'.

6. The actors are now allowed to interact with all of the characters using real words.
7. The group returns to the circle and are put into smaller groups to create a symbolic image of power. The participants should ignore their given number for this stage of the activity. Each image will be performed for the rest of the group to observe.

8. The actors return to the circle and are put into new groups of eight so that every number is represented. These groups must make an image of a real-life situation of power relationships between these characters. These images will again be shared and interpreted by the rest of the group.

Example of situations explored by Jana Sanskriti are:

- Economically marginalised people being exiled from their home by government members.

- A hospital with people in various positions of power.

- A political leader, the bureaucrats, the Panchayat (local government) and villagers at the same point in one day.

Workshop 3

Exercise 1: Forum in a circle

1. The group are divided into subgroups of three in order to develop a short role-play based on oppression. The role-play must be based on a realistic oppressive situation. One performer should take on the role of an oppressed person, another person should play the oppressor and the final person should play the role of someone who is trying and failing to help the oppressed character.

2. Each group will perform their scene to an audience three times. Each time the group performs the scene, they should switch roles so that each performer has the opportunity to play every role. It is important that every time the play is performed, new ideas are generated rather than simply repeating what another performer has said. This is in order to discover new dimensions in the content.
3. After the group has swapped the roles, they should use that experience in order to develop their forum scene with the ideas generated from swapping roles. They should be given five to ten minutes.

4. These scenes should be shared with the group in a circle, whilst the other groups are frozen in their starting position. Examples of the scenes created by Jana Sanskriti are: a woman trying to report a rape to the police who dismiss her. A sick woman needs treatment and is trying to be convinced to pay money to go to a private hospital. A family who are trying to report to a police officer that their daughter has been trafficked; the policeman blames the family for sending their daughter to work at the age of fourteen and refuses to help.

5. After each group has shared their developed scene, the protagonist from each group moves counter-clockwise so that they are now the protagonist in a new situation. Each group should perform again, with the new protagonist, who should use different tactics in order to try and change the situation and combat the oppressor.

6. Once every group has performed again, protagonists should move to the next group in the circle and try a new tactic in their new role. This step should be repeated a few times in order to explore each problem in a different way each time. During this process, the facilitator should clap his/her hands to stop and start each scene to control the pace of the performance and to move swiftly between each group.

Exercise 2: Variation on Columbian hypnosis

(Boal, *Games* . . ., p. 63)

1. In pairs, one person will lead the other with the palm of the hand so that the face is 10 cm away from it. It is important to keep the distance between the palm of the hand of the leader and the follower's face constant. In order for this to be possible it is also important for the hypnotist to move at a slow pace to fully hypnotise the follower. The hypnotised member should be prepared to move his/her body in any shape in order to follow the leader's hand. At any point, if the facilitator claps, the pairs should freeze in their positions. A second clap allows the pairs to move again.
2. At a point where the pairs are frozen, the facilitator can choose two or three striking images and ask the rest of the group to observe them one by one. The facilitator can deepen his/her exploration by asking questions such as: 'who has the power here?'; 'who are the characters?'; 'what power situation does this remind you of?' This helps to ground the spectator's interpretations in reality. Examples of power relationships found by Jana Sanskriti are: a teacher and a student; a city dweller and a villager; a father and a daughter.
3. After exploring the images, the actors should return to their partners and continue the hypnosis exercise in the same roles. The facilitator can continue stopping and starting the action with claps through the activity, which should take place for at least ten minutes.

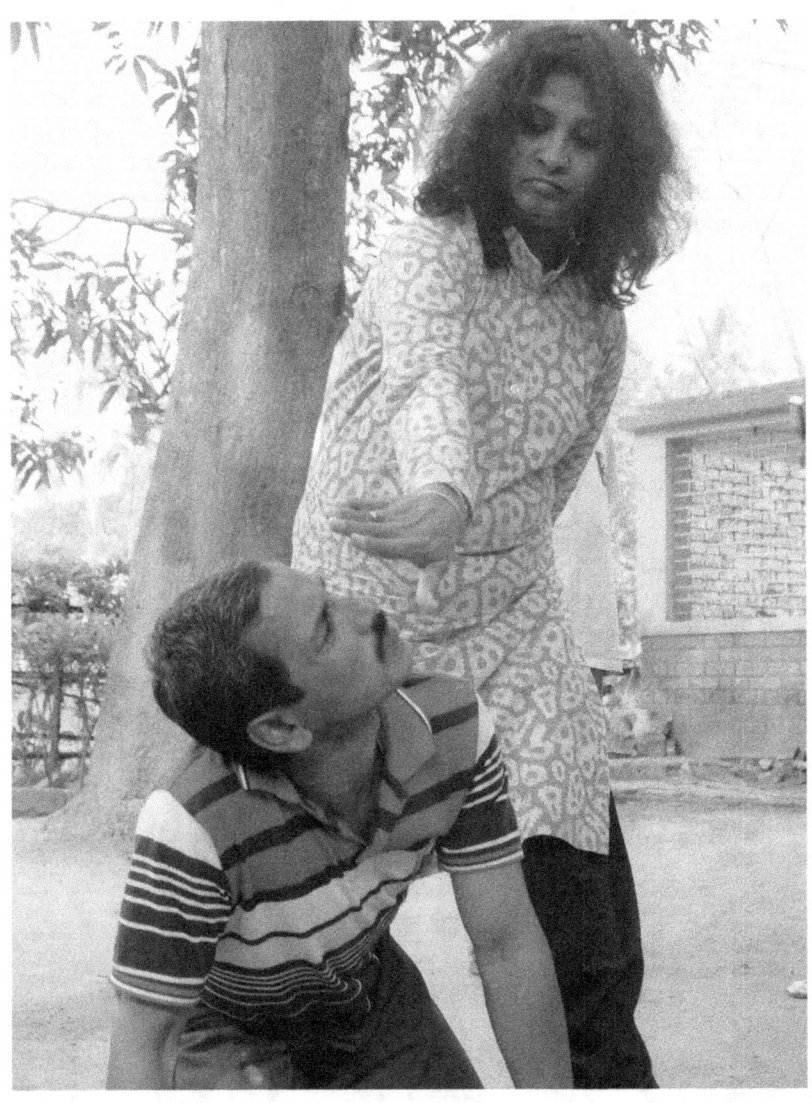

4. Next, the actors should form two lines on each side of the rehearsal space facing away from each other. On one side are those who led the hypnosis, on the other are the participants who were led. The facilitator tells them to collect their feelings of being in the exercise, whether they were in control of power or powerless. When they are ready, the participants should turn around and reflect that feeling in a symbolic image as an individual.

5. One by one, the participants should come to the centre of the space with their original hypnosis partner and share their images at the same time. When the facilitator claps, the pair should improvise dialogue that reflects a situation with an oppressor and an oppressed. Examples from Jana Sanskriti are: a trafficker pressuring a prostitute into submission; a landlord taking advantage of a poor tenant; a woman from a doctor's family chastising a villager for calling a doctor too early in the morning.

Variation 2: Columbian hypnosis

1. The group are put into subgroups of three and numbered from 1 to 3. Number 1's should hypnotise the two other group members using both hands. Similar to the previous hypnosis activity, both followers should be led around the space, exploring different levels at a slow pace.

2. On the facilitator's clap the members of the group rotate so that number 2 becomes the leader. After some time, number 3 is able to lead so that each person has the experience of both leading and following. This activity should be completed in silence. The facilitator can continue freezing the action using a clap as a signal.
3. After this activity has been explored for a while, the participants should return to the circle. They are asked to consider one word that describes how they felt during the game.
4. When everyone has chosen a word, the actors should walk around the space in circular movements, sharing their words with other group members as they walk past each other. The participants should aim to hear everyone's words to get a holistic view of everyone's experiences.
5. The actors are put into groups of five. Using one of the actors' words, each group should create a frozen picture which portrays a realistic situation inspired by the chosen word.

6. The actors should share their images one by one and the spectators should try and guess the word. Examples of words chosen by Jana Sanskriti are "pain", "reality" and "why".

Note: Boal's focus is mainly on physical flexibility, whereas as always Ganguly's opens the exercise out into the development of feelings and an exploration of what they signal about social and political realities.

Exercise 3: Blind game

(Similar to Boal's 'The blind series' [*Games*, pp. 106–7])

The group is organised into pairs. One member of each pair closes his/her eyes. The other person moves around the space, whispering his/her partner's name: the blind partner follows the voice, and it is the job of the person that can see to keep the other safe.

1. After some time, the partner that can see stops moving and continues whispering the blind partner's name. This allows the partners to come into contact.

2. Keeping their eyes closed, all actors should then separate and weave throughout the other actors, feeling everyone's hands and arms. When they feel they have come into contact with their original partner, they should freeze together, keeping their eyes closed.
3. All actors should then close their eyes. In their pairs, they should feel the arms and hands of their partners carefully, paying attention to the details that make these hands individual.

Workshop 3   63

4. When all the actors have paired up, the facilitator instructs them to open their eyes and find out if they have succeeded in finding their partner.
5. The actors can now stand in a circle. A few individuals are chosen to stand in the middle of the circle. These actors are blindfolded. One by one, the actors in the circle can run into the middle and tap the blindfolded actors. When they feel contact, the blindfolded ones in the middle should try and catch the person who touched them. If they succeed, they feel the arms and

hands of the person they have caught and try to identify them. If they are correct, the two actors swap and the caught person becomes blindfolded.

Exercise 4: Storytelling

1. In groups of three, actors will sit back to back so that they are not facing each other but are touching. One member of the group tells a story of oppression from real life. It doesn't have to be a story they are directly involved in but it must be a story they know of from real life. The others can ask questions to clarify their understanding of the story. A second member of the group tells another story: within the group the best story is chosen.

2. The troupe make an audience, and one group take the stage to share their story. One member tells the story verbally with hands behind the back, another member stands behind the storyteller with hands on hips so that during the story the hands are free to express it. To create the illusion that it is one body, a scarf can be placed over the shoulders of the storyteller. The third person acts the story out with his/her body and takes on different characters in the story, using the whole body and facial expressions to represent it without words.

3. After the story is told, two spectators create an image of the story they have just heard using other spectators. The original group observes the two images and chooses the image that best represents their story or synthesises the two; they are also able to make small changes to the image to make it more accurate.

4. When the final image has been determined, the next group will share their story in the same way. The process will continue so that all groups are able to share their stories.

5. An example of a story told at Jana Sanskriti is of a headmaster who is harassed by the villagers of the area in which he teaches due to his poor teaching standards. He goes to the police, who come to the school, which frightens the children and leads to their abandoning the school. In this story, it is the students that suffer due to their lack of education.

Workshop 4

Note: Many of the exercises in this section start from ways of working together to develop forms and textures and levels of interaction in the process of creating a scene; they are always targeted towards collaborative creation.

Exercise 1: Catch in the circle

1. The group stand in a circle. Everyone faces to the left, so they can only see each others' backs. One person begins the game by pushing the participant in front of him/her gently and taking that space as the person steps forward. The person who has stepped forward does the same, and so the company begins slowly rotating.
2. When the movement has its flow, one participant begins the second movement by pushing the person two in front of him and taking his or her place when the person steps forward. This person does the same, and so two movements are now present in the circle. The aim is for both movements to maintain a steady flow. The exercise is a good warm-up that promotes special awareness and concentration.

Exercise 2: Newspaper theatre

1. Groups of about four or five are formed, depending on the number of participants. The groups each choose a story or picture from a newspaper. As groups, they discuss it and create a still image from it.
2. After some time, the groups each present their images to the other participants. This is done by the groups standing in a circle and holding their images while others focus their attention on each one by one.

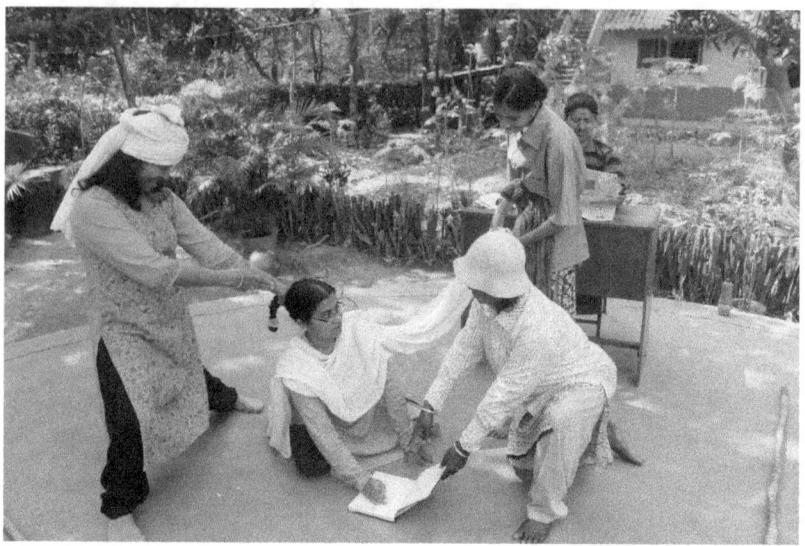

3. Each group then observes the group opposite them in the circle in order to work out what news story it is based on. If no one in the group recognises a news story in the image, they can make it up. The groups then each create a new image based on their interpretation of the image of the group opposite them in the circle. Initially their task is to create a short scene using no sound.
4. One by one, the groups showcase their interpretation to the rest of the group, starting with their still image and adding movement on the facilitator's clap. After the next clap, the group should add text and sound to their play.

5. After observing the others' performances, the audience should discuss the news stories explored and what issues are brought up by them.

Exercise 3: Points of contact

1. Groups of five are formed. The facilitator brings their attention to the fact that each group has ten points of contact with the floor: their ten feet. The facilitator challenges them to remove one point of contact within the group on each of his claps: from ten to nine, eight, seven, six, five, four and so on. When each group has reached the minimum points of contact they can manage, they share it with the group.

2. The facilitator then asks them to try having the same number of points of contact with the ground, but to use a different strategy, for example a knee and two feet instead of two hands and a foot.
3. After this, the group comes into a circle. The facilitator asks the groups to give the exercise a title that is no longer than one sentence. Jana Sanskriti's groups had names such as "support", "take care of me", "combination of power" and "trust and intimacy". As a whole ensemble, the group can then choose one as the best name for the exercise. This activity allows the participants to use ingenuity in the task and to practise teamwork while facing challenges.

Exercise 4: Invisible friend

1. An empty chair is placed in front of an audience. One of the participants enters the space and starts a mimed conversation with an invisible person and in doing so creates a situation. When another participant has imagined who this person could be, he or she enters the space and mimes with the other, illustrating the situation. They keep playing without words.
2. When they feel it is appropriate, another participant can enter the stage and begin miming in order to develop the situation.

3. When the facilitator claps, they improvise dialogue.

4. When the facilitator feels the scene has developed sufficiently, they clap and a final frozen image should be created by the actors. In this example almost all the participants had entered the stage throughout the exercise.

5. This exercise can be developed by adding more props on to the stage, which the participants can improvise with – they can be used in a literal or metaphorical sense; for example, a microphone can be used as a microphone, a telephone, a teacup or a mouse.

Exercise 5: Soundscape and images

1. Groups of six are formed. The facilitator instructs the groups to create a soundscape that reflects any situation: a storm, a train station, a city scene or a kitchen, for example. The groups should be given ten minutes to prepare the soundscape.
2. The groups should stand in a circle. One group performs their soundscape while the rest of the participants close their eyes and listen.
3. Immediately after they have heard the noise, the participants should create a still image in their groups that reflects the sound they have heard. Only minimal discussion is allowed. Each image should be viewed by the rest of the group.

4. After all the sounds have been performed and multiple images have been created, all participants of the workshop should explain what they interpreted from the soundscape so that it can be discovered whether the creators of the soundscapes gave an accurate portrayal of the scenario they envisaged. After critical discussion, the groups of six can go away and try to improve their work.
5. The groups share their improved work and the audience criticise.

6. Examples of soundscapes created by Jana Sanskriti are:
   a. A woman is abandoned by her husband at a train station.
   b. There is a storm the night before a bride's wedding. When she leaves in the morning, the family are sad.
   c. A woman is raped on a boat and no one else on board notices because they are singing.

d. Everyone is dancing to techno at a Puja festival; an old man is seriously ill but no one notices as they are dancing and distracted.

Exercise 6: Characters' stories

1. Groups of six are formed. In the centre of a circle, put lots of pieces of paper with characters written on them, for example: policeman, mother, thief. Every participant should choose a piece of paper so that everyone will have a character. The groups then have to create a short silent scene based on a story between the characters they have been given.
2. After some time, the groups should come back to the circle and perform their short silent scene. The audience should guess what each person's character was from the action they see.
3. Examples of the stories Jana Sanskriti created are:
   a. A husband goes to market, leaving his wife and cleaner at home. He gets drunk and meets a man who is very promiscuous. A thief steals the necklace of a woman the promiscuous man has just been with. The husband catches the thief and discovers that it was his wife's chain.
   b. A farmer works hard all day and gets home to find his son watching television. He scolds his son. He then finds out that his wife has become pregnant and scolds her and leaves the house to fume on the street. A beggar comes and they speak; a transgender person arrives, intending to bless the baby, but the farmer turns him away. A political leader comes and appeals to the farmer, who has no money to give him. The baby is born.

c. A woman is seriously ill but she and her family can't get to the hospital due to traffic jams in the city caused by a political rally.

d. The minister comes to an agreement with an agricultural company about their production of seeds. The minister asks a bureaucrat to distribute the seeds in his area. The bureaucrat doesn't comply, so the minister pays hoodlums to beat him.

Workshop 5

Exercise 1: Moving as a still image

The participants stand in a circle with their eyes closed. The facilitator asks each individual to create an image of oppression with his/her body. Keeping their eyes closed and moving only their feet, the participants should move around the space carefully.

1. The participants should feel for other participants in order to form groups of five or six. This exercise increases special awareness and concentration.
2. In their groups, participants should open their eyes and share with each other their images of oppression. Each group chooses their favourite image.
3. Using this image as inspiration, the participants should create a short scene without dialogue. For this they are allowed fifteen minutes.
4. The groups should share their stories with the rest of the participants, one by one. After each performance, the group should talk about what they have seen and speak critically about both the stories and their subject matters.

Exercise 2: Experiencing the lives of others

1. In a circle facing outwards, the participants are instructed by the facilitator to imagine a person they know in real life. When the participants are ready, they should turn around and create an individual image that represents this person.

Workshop 5 81

2. On the facilitator's clap, the participants should move around the space portraying their image of the real person. When they meet another

participant, they should swap images so that they can experience harnessing the image of another character. The exercise can only finish when every participant has portrayed every image. This gives participants practice at creating different images and an exposure to various characters.

Exercise 3: Glass Cobra becomes the Trade Union Game

1. This game is inspired by Boal's game Glass Cobra (*Games*, p. 108), but Jana Sanskriti has named it the Trade Union Game. The participants stand in a circle. All of them turn right and hold the shoulders of the person in front with both of their hands. They should feel the head, hair, face and shoulders of the person in front of them.
2. Then everyone should close their eyes and bring their hands to their sides. The facilitator tells them that they are a trade union that is about to be divided because they have closed their eyes. Their closed eyes symbolise their submission and lack of awareness of political parties infiltrating their union.
3. Now the facilitator moves individual participants to various corners of the room. They must keep their eyes closed. The facilitator can give examples such as: you've been won over by the communists, you have become a socialist, you are in the labour party, you are with the conservatives, etc. Ultimately, the trade union becomes completely separated and each individual is isolated.
4. The facilitator informs the participants that they are no longer a united workers' front, that they have been divided. To reunite, they must search with their eyes closed for the person that was previously in front of them in order to re-achieve the circle they were originally a part of.
5. When the participants have reformed the circle as it was, the participants and the facilitator should then talk about how this game relates to society. The discussion will encourage them to think critically and engage with current political issues.

Part 2
Interviews with Sanjoy Ganguly and short essays

Introductory note

In the following section, Sanjoy Ganguly, Jana Sanskriti's artistic director, responds to some questions about how he has developed this methodology and what its underlying premises and goals are. This section draws on material from several interviews conducted with him over the last few years; three short pieces by Ganguly conclude the section. In some cases minor corrections and rephrasings have been made by the editor.

Some of the issues and themes which Ganguly discusses are:

1. Games as social metaphors
2. Scripting the play
3. Relationship, connection and process
4. Forum and intervention: plays as debate-structures; the cultivation of rationality
5. Spectactors and spect-activism
6. The role of the joker
7. Aesthetics
8. TO in the context of the market economy
9. 'Development', participation and agency

****

Interview 1
Interview with Sima and Sanjoy Ganguly, November 2013

Conducted by Robert Klement

The interviewees are members and founders of the India-based cultural movement 'Jana Sanskriti', which works through Theatre of the Oppressed to equip people to fight against their daily oppressions, and organisers of the biannual international Theatre of the Oppressed festival 'Muktadhara' in Calcutta, India. Sanjoy Ganguly has published various books on scripting power and practising freedom on and offstage.

'About the rehearsal for total revolution and the practice of love'

Robert: What is Jana Sanskriti today, in 2013?

Sanjoy: Today, Jana Sanskriti is a political space for marginalised people; a space that allows them to talk and develop an understanding about their issues. It's a democratic space for doing politics through theatre, where people script power in theatre and in collective action. More and more this power is being applied by actors and spectators in real life, so they become '*spect-activists*', as I love to say.

People have the urge to be the rational thinkers and participants in the construction of human society. They don't only talk about their immediate issues but also about policies.

We are now doing Forum theatre on the education system where we talk about the problems of the system. People are coming up with their own perspective as to how the education system should be structured. In the process of debate they develop an understanding of the issue and they suggest how to reconstruct and radically reformulate the system. So people are no longer just implementing agencies of the policies created by the system – they are now drafting policies. So we have taken theatre to a level where people are really in the process of constructing human society.

Sima: From 1985, the year Jana Sanskriti was born, to today our family has extended. Jana Sanskriti is not the name of an organisation or an institution, Jana Sanskriti is a large family. At this moment, there are about 500–600 actors and actresses.

Robert: So Jana Sanskriti is not just an organisation but it's a big movement. Why do you think Jana Sanskriti is so successful?

Sanjoy: First of all we recognise the intellectual abilities of people. They need to exercise the intellectual rights that they are deprived of. People cannot be satisfied with only bread, butter and salt. Intellect is something that human beings have and they don't want to be neglected on that question. When their intellect is recognised and when they develop as rational and thoughtful citizens, they see it as their job to continue this movement. Secondly, we developed a strategy of being present in the community on a continuous and consistent basis. The teams are evolving from the community; they perform in their own villages. After being present over years and years they develop a connection with the spectators.

So Jana Sanskriti fundamentally thinks that people are essentially intellectual and secondly that Theatre of the Oppressed is a politics of creating connection. Those two foundations allow people to get connected to our movement, to this theatre and towards transforming society. We have developed a truly democratic relationship with the spectators and therefore we are a big movement today.

Sima: *I become we, we become they.* We are not just saying this in front of people. We are practising it. That's why, I think, we have a feeling of collectiveness. There are members of our group who have been part of this family for twenty years; the youngest ones have been here for sixteen, seventeen years.

We are not talking from our heads; we are talking from our hearts.

Sanjoy always says that the time *you* go to direct a workshop you are cultivating your 'I'. This way, you cannot destroy hierarchy, and the workshop cannot become a space for real dialogue. For us, it is the '*we*' that conducts a theatre workshop. I am not 'I'. This is what we practise in our group also. That's why I think Jana Sanskriti, as Boal used to say, is 'the largest Theatre of the Oppressed movement in the world'.

If someone becomes part of Jana Sanskriti, his or her whole family becomes part of Jana Sanskriti. That's why our family is really large, a really big family. Your parents are suffering from illness – that means our parents are suffering from illness. This spirit makes us come together and we try to grow it more and more.

Robert: Boal called the Theatre of the Oppressed a 'rehearsal for revolution'; nowadays we often say a 'rehearsal for reality'. In Jana Sanskriti you say it's a 'rehearsal for the total revolution'. What does that mean?

Sanjoy: With total revolution we mean people evolving as intellectuals. When actors and spectators develop a sociological understanding of their issues, they experience intellectual growth. That is what we call internal revolution. That breaks the passivity. That inspires them to go for an external revolution. So we are saying it's a total revolution.

The internal revolution is important for the external revolution. If the external revolution happens without the internal revolution, you are speaking *for* the people instead of letting them speak for themselves. It is important that everyone experiences this internal revolution. The Theatre of the Oppressed movement should take care of both aspects, internal and external revolution.

I define this internal revolution as the Aesthetics of Theatre of the Oppressed. What you see in our theatre is the structural beauty – but when people in connection discuss and evolve together, they experience the aesthetics.[1] Internal revolution breaks self-interest. It means liberation from 'I'. That is why internal revolution is what we need to transform society and to create real collective action.

Robert: Do you think this is possible in the Western world, which is very much based on 'I'?

Sanjoy: It's very much based on 'I'. I can see that people suffer from this pain of being individualistic. But the suffering because of 'I' is also understood by people. So maybe there are still ways waiting to be discovered. We have to have optimism in our heart and something will definitely happen.

Often I am told by my Theatre of the Oppressed friends that people in the West do not talk about their oppressions. I don't think this is the fault of the people; it is caused by social conditioning. Most people live in alienation and isolation. Being always inside the invisible fence of individualism, they experience a disconnection. That reflects in the workshop; they cannot feel connected easily, and therefore they hide the real story that affects them. We must understand that and we need to know how we can deal with this phenomenon.

Sima: Without practice you don't get success. If you study mathematics you need to practise mathematics. And if you love someone, you should practise the same way, right from your heart. Don't only see people as short-term relations. If you genuinely practise that connection, then you don't forget how to use it. It is true.

Robert: What do you think is the biggest challenge for Theatre of the Oppressed and its community in these days?

Sanjoy: It's a big question to me if the Theatre of the Oppressed community is a community or not because being in a community means the continuous sharing of thoughts, ideas and practices. You would not have to buy them as commodity. Sometimes I see that people buy the techniques and that creates a market. On one hand we criticise the market; on the other hand we create a market. Our head and heart are not always connected. Recognising this is a part of the internal revolution.

The problem is that theatrical means are slowly slowly going into the hands of the privileged people and not into the hands of the underprivileged people at the margin. We must work on that and we must shout out loud. Of course, theatre is my profession but at the same time I am responsible to hand over the theatrical means of production to the underprivileged people. So working on this difference in practice and in what we preach is something that Theatre of the Oppressed is not doing as a community. Are we cultivating the rational thinking of the oppressed class or developing masters ('experts') who love to direct workshops – this is a big question. Sometimes I hear people saying they direct workshops, they don't say they are facilitating them.

Secondly, I think that Theatre of the Oppressed is based on a cultural dialogue – but often there are multiple monologues because everybody thinks he is right. This dogma inside this movement sometimes makes me wild. If we only keep maintaining our own positions as a dogma, then we are negating the concept of dialogue and debate in Theatre of the Oppressed. That is the most worrying fact to me. We must create a space where we should speak with our hearts in order to understand each other and in order to develop it [*Theatre of the Oppressed*], in order to go beyond where Boal has stopped. Instead, if we think we have the legacy and we are teachers, then this will definitely cause problems in Theatre of the Oppressed. Then we won't be able to create rational thinkers, instead we will create followers. Even though we're talking about collective action, we are not really practising it. That happened in every movement, even in the Marxist movement and in the socialist bloc. They found some leaders, some new form of rulers. That is why they didn't last. If Theatre of the Oppressed continues in this direction, it will have problems.

Robert: In the twenty-eight years of the existence of Jana Sanskriti, is there a moment that you consider as special?

Sanjoy: That's the most difficult question.

Sima: There are plenty. How can I mention just one?

In 2006, Boal visited Jana Sanskriti and addressed a Spectactors Rally where 12,000 spectators came from different villages. I saw Boal's face shining. It was a strong feeling to see his happiness. He cried. It was a wonderful day.

Two years later Boal died but he is very much with us. We did everything from his inspiration. 'Jana Sanskriti is the largest movement in this world.' This sentence makes me feel that we really did something.

It was a special moment, a special day.

Sanjoy: It's special for all of us. When I say that Theatre of the Oppressed will not be a doctrine, that – like all philosophies – it has a lot of opportunities to go further, it's actually the best way of showing respect to Boal. Sometimes people do not understand this. I have seen the way it has influenced me, so now it is my responsibility to develop it. And that's how we pay respect to Boal. You should have seen his face in the rally! Boal at times also tried to support us financially. In March 2009 before he passed away he wrote to me stating: 'you will not retire from TO, Theatre of the Oppressed needs you!! If you have any despair, dump it on me'. I considered those words as the best award in my career.

And there was also the moment when there were multiple crises in Jana Sanskriti. In 1997, we lost the support of an NGO that used to support us. It was a big crisis. We thought that probably this movement will go no further. But surprisingly from 1997 to 2000 we received so much support from people. That helped us and the crisis couldn't break Jana Sanskriti. We didn't know that our work had so much value for the people!

Robert: Thank you for this interview!

Note

1 For more discussion of Ganguly's view of aesthetics, see the following interview (pp. 92, 95) and the concluding essays, especially those on p. 133ff and p. 142ff.

Interview 2
Interview with Sanjoy Ganguly, 30 July 2013

Conducted by Robyn Kirkby

Robyn: Many of Jana Sanskriti's (JS) plays depict women's struggle in society. How did you create those plays as a company? What was the process that led up to the end product?

Sanjoy: In all the plays, we follow the method that we call 'scripting the play'. When I first decided to be a theatre person I formed a theatre group in a village with the local youth, and it was all men because women were not allowed to perform, whereas now more than 50 percent of the actors in JS are women, even amongst the jokers. When I was working with the group in the beginning of JS I noticed that if they were asked to *play a script* it was too taxing for them because they cannot read, they are hearing and trying to memorise. In folk theatre, actually they don't often 'play the script' they 'script the play'. I noticed this, so therefore I decided to approach from a different angle and let them script the play, because if they script the play themselves they will be able to remember. So that is how JS playmaking started.

Later on it was filtered, we developed more after becoming in touch with Boal. The methodology of Theatre of the Oppressed (TO) helped us to allow the participants to be spectators of their own reality. So basically, Boal's method is about opening doors; enlarging, magnifying the reality so they can discover the tiny elements within it. We also see games as social metaphors; they are a bridge between participants inside the room and the reality outside; it connects. So people cultivate their reality. While cultivating what is there in the reality, they discover what is oppression, who is the oppressor, how do the oppressed think; they are either submissive or they want to protest. So the theatre workshops become a sociology class. Actors understand, before they go before the audience, they analyse the problem from a social science point of view. So that is why even the process is very important in TO. People often neglect the process, but it is, if not more than, equally as important as the product. JS is essentially Theatre *of* the Oppressed; they make the story themselves. They act in the performance; it's not Theatre *for* the Oppressed.

In the case of women, in the workshop they saw their reality, so they made images of their reality, of their family. They understood in the workshop how patriarchy functions. The director's role is to structure it, is to add the aesthetic value in it. But the scripts come, essentially, from the participants. Women saw their lives in the workshop, their reality, they studied the scripted images, they scripted dialogues, and that's how they play. You can see in *Golden Girl* it is a combination of Forum and image theatre; there are a lot of images there because the text was not very important. They came up with a lot of images because women in the villages habitually were not used to speaking much, but they were comfortable scripting images. This is why you can see that image plays a major role in all of our plays. It's the image, combined with text.

Robyn: My next question is specific to the play *Sarama*. At the end of the play the chorus speaks directly to the audience about the causes of gender inequality and questions them on what needs to change. For example: 'We need war against patriarchy' and 'We must begin the fight within the family'. Could you tell me a bit about how that was received and how the audience responded to those direct questions?

Sanjoy: In this play, we have addressed the broader question of how the position of women has developed through various processes in the society. It is about a rape before the election, so for the political parties it was more about how to use this against the ruling party, and for the ruling party the important thing was to suppress the matter. The position adopted towards this issue of rape is in order to expose the patriarchal nature of the political parties. Sometimes those parties are even led by women. We always say that patriarchy is an ideology and it can be followed by women too. I have seen a lot of female patriarchy in my life. Patriarchy has nothing to do with being a man or woman. Margaret Thatcher, she was a patriarch! This is what we wanted to expose. The other thing is that inside most Indian political organisations the women's wing is always controlled by the men. In the communist party, where we see that the party in power is trying to suppress the opposition, they are directing the women's wing to save the respect of the party; the question is not how the woman got raped by the men. The women's wing cannot have independence, the party will control them. In most cases, the political forces have a women's wing, which they control. We are questioning the whole system of controlling a target group.

Also, we questioned that if there was not an NGO, how could she (Sarama) survive in this society? Sarama's empowerment came about because she was supported by an NGO. Without this support she wouldn't have been able to achieve it. This was made very clear by some tribal women who work in the mines where they cut stones. Initially, the end of the play was different; we wanted to show a successful empowered woman. But the tribal women came over after the play was finished and they told us, 'what you have shown in your play is good, as the woman is very empowered' and we said 'yes, don't you think so?' Then they said 'look, we work in the mines, under a contractor and it is an open secret that the contractor calls us to his room and we have to go. If we don't go we lose our job. And people know, everyone knows, so we get raped every day. Do you think we are empowered?' That was their question. And so we had absolutely no answer. These people are so strong, running their family (the men are mostly idle), they earn money, they cook, they look after their children, they look after guests like our theatre group, and everything they do with a laughing mood, they are never depressed. Depression is a luxury. They experience this sort of torture from the men, aggressive patriarchy they experience every day. So then we thought: 'no, this is not what we should actually show in the play'. So we changed the ending so the actors then put the question: how is this possible? We realised that it is not the case that an NGO will always come and liberate you; the fight should begin from the family, the men have a role in it. That since the men will have a role, at the end we asked our audience, what do you think about it? We still have no answer. This is actually how we jumped into Forum theatre. We realised that we cannot pass any judgement.

Robyn: How did the men in the audience react to these questions?

Sanjoy: When they were asking the questions, actually there were no men around us on that particular occasion. The men left after the play was over, but the women came forward and they were very courageous women.

We realised that within the play there were several opportunities to forum, like the whole political question of the women's wing.

We have also done forums about the time when the rape is taking place, because the neighbours' role was very passive and this gave people the opportunity to intervene in these roles. Actually, the play was so sensational that it created a debate. Some people said that under an authoritarian, regimented party supported by the police, these criminals are supported by the political party and the police and it is difficult to fight them. Other people said, but if there is no attempt we cannot make our voices heard to the ruling party. It is a debate and that is what we wanted; with Forum theatre JS always thinks that it is not the question of solving the problem on stage. Some people see it as a problem solving session, but how do you solve a question of patriarchy on stage? In a play? It is an age-old problem, you have to fight against it for years. So, therefore it is not a question of solving, the purpose is to disturb the mind of the people, the purpose is to create confusion, contradictions, and also some convictions. But they should go with conflicts, debate. This debate actually allows an intellectual growth. JS thinks that people are essentially intellectual, but they don't realise it. However, this intellectual capacity is not always manifested because of the political forces, they are always told to follow. Even the NGO culture, on this continent, works by saying: 'you don't know anything, *you* follow *me*'. The participants are fake participants: 'you have to say things that we want you to say'. That's the sort of participatory approach some NGOs take, so in that way they are following the same way as party politics where people are following them. People's rational intellectual growth is what needs to be manifested, and that is real development. So, when people debate, when they are engaged in a debate (debate means they want to find their way), they are coming closer to each other. But if you are dogmatic, it alienates, because everybody is trying to win. But in Forum theatre, nobody is trying to *win*. Everyone is trying to find ways to address the issue, so it is a process of convergence, it is a form which fights alienation. Suppose you are portraying a scene of domestic violence: a husband is beating his wife, without any rhyme or reason. So the audience initially will think it's a problem between a husband and a wife, then: 'oh it is a problem between a man and a woman, it's a problem inside a family'; then slowly, slowly, as the argument proceeds, Forum theatre can lead them to understand that it is not a question of a family, it is not a problem between a man and a woman: it is the problem of patriarchy. Patriarchy is acting as an ideology in the psyche of the oppressor. So from a scene of domestic violence, they are developing an understanding about patriarchy.

Everyone thinks that the joker is very important, but the joker is not important. The actors and the oppressive characters are important in order to problematise. The oppressor character problematises as he acts with his ideology, and the spect-actor comes to contradict him. This contradiction raises questions, and people follow those questions, people try to address those questions that evolve in the argument. When they keep questioning, understanding grows farther and farther, and they understand that it's actually patriarchy.

It is important to play the same play in front of the same audience at least three times with an interval. Sometimes we do it five times, in front of the same audience, the same play. Usually we leave one month, three weeks in between performances. People go with a conflict and next time they intervene with a more critical approach, so this is how they develop this understanding. It's an intellectual journey, from experience to the cause, from the result to the reason. In this journey, actors and spectators, they grow intellectually. And when they experience intellectual growth they experience the aesthetics of their lives. That's the aesthetics to me, it is not what my play looks like, I call that 'structural beauty', but aesthetic is when actors and spectators feel the intellectual growth in them, which I call 'internal revolution'. This internal revolution inspires people because they are intellectually growing, thinking rationally and logically they try to act in their real life. So in real life when they act, then I call it 'spect-activism'. Boal said spect-actor, and now we are saying spect-activists. This internal revolution inspires people to go for external revolution, external transformation, they act in their real lives with a logical, rational position. That is spect-activism.

Robyn: When did you decide to perform the same play multiple times to the same audience?

Sanjoy: First of all the idea came when we addressed an alcohol issue in the village, and when we addressed the alcohol issue, then we found that people were coming up with very aggressive interventions. So then we thought about why people are getting so violent, so then we thought that we should go another time. Going the next time we saw that people are becoming more rational. So they are trying to formulate strategies as to how to fight against it. They understood that with violence we cannot achieve success, so we have to be tactical addressing the triangular nexus between the liquor lobby, police and dishonest political leaders.

We realised the strength of taking the same play to the same audience time and again. When they first come to watch it, I call it 'joint social action' because they try to intervene but it's a joint social action. When they come a second time, meanwhile they have been reflecting. After the reflection they feel the need to be connected with others. Actually, the second time when they come as spect-actors it becomes 'collective action'. To go from joint social action to collective action you should give them some time to reflect, which helps them to understand the value of being connected. When they get connected, everybody's brain comes together; we see that the participation becomes very strong. When we see at the end of the play that people are still debating, that there is some sort of incompleteness, then we feel that we should perform the play again, then more people will intervene. When we see that people are not debating much, not debating as a group, then we think that we can stop.

Each time, we decide to end the play at a point where people will feel dissatisfied. When they feel there needs to be more time to talk about it, *then* we finish; deliberately, quite strategically. The next time we go, people feel like talking more but by then they have thought about it.

Robyn: The play *Where We Stand* describes lots of the interventions for 'The Brick Factory' as either magical or conservative and you are quoted saying that there isn't an actual realistic solution to Phulmoni's problem. Why do you continue to perform a play if you don't think there is a solution. What is the benefit of this?

Sanjoy: When we perform this play in front of the community, we want to raise the question, who is at fault? So our idea was to disturb people by that question. There is an intervention point when there is a discussion about whether women should get equal wages to men or not, then there is another intervening point when the contractor is calling at Phulmoni's house in the night, here we do a lot of forum. But when the trial comes, then it is true that, in the tribal system, people find it hard to act against the Village Head who thinks that Phulmoni is at fault, that she has spoilt our village, that she has spoilt the nature of our culture, so she should be punished. They don't talk about the contractor. In a tribal tradition, it is difficult to challenge the Village Head, there are a lot of good things but also a lot of beliefs and superstitions in that community. When we have the same play in non-tribal communities, then they actually can

	raise questions. If you go to the villages where we have been working for a long time, people are in many ways different from any standard Indian village. There they can take up the issue because they challenge an authority often, because they are already so empowered that they are used to talking against the authority.

Robyn: Has the Village Head ever come to one of your performances?

Sanjoy: Yes, they sometimes come and we have experienced that when they are in the audience they try and create problems, they want to terrorise, but when we performed this play there was an organisation behind those tribal people, an activist movement which has a stronghold in that area. Without that organisation, these people could have caused an issue. But now, times are changing – but in that particular scene when she is on trial, we don't do much forum on it there. Because the Village Head, with all his power, makes it difficult to do something. So we discuss about equal wages and why the contractor is coming and we raise this issue of how can the contractor be innocent, why should he not be put on trial? So that is the question, and if the question itself makes them think, then that is the point, no matter how many interventions come.

Sometimes forum is measured through the number of interventions, but suppose you are performing a play in Afghanistan – you can't expect that a woman would come to the stage and do something about it, but do you think we are not making them think? So you can't always judge the success of a piece by the number of interventions that have taken place. It is how much disturbance it is creating, how much it is inspiring them to think. *That* is the parameter of success.

If you go to JS's old area where three generations of people are watching, it is the only place in the world where you can see grandfather, father and son, three generations watching Forum theatre. From when we first went into the villages, the forty-year-old man is now sixty-seven years and he has a son of thirty-five years, and that child has a son of fourteen years. There they are so used to intervening, the joker doesn't really have to work, as they will just come and try. But is it creating a debate? Is it problematising the situation? Is it helping people to understand pros and cons? Is it responsible for any kind of intellectual development? Only then will they take action in their real lives – otherwise there is no point.

Robyn: In the past twenty-seven years JS has expanded a lot. Do you think in another twenty-seven years the newer communities will reach the same degree of empowerment as the villages that you have just mentioned?

Sanjoy: I don't know actually, because after working for more than a quarter of a century I often feel tired. It depends on the ground-level leadership and others in JS, because I don't want to work more actually. JS is already so cultivated and known, it has generated so much interest in the country that automatically it is spreading. The only big challenge is that to organise money is so difficult, and if you are challenging the authority, no government is happy with this, so we are getting no government money. We also don't want to depend on institutional grants – that is why now we try and expand through organisations that already exist there, so we won't have to take care of everything, they can take care of their team. But those organisations are also in financial crisis, they are also not getting support, because if you don't follow the agendas of the donors, then you get no money. That is becoming a pressure more and more – the institutions are dictating and they don't want people to be organised. The activist movement is suffering, as they are getting no money, and the more it is weakening the more we are finding it difficult. Through established people, NGOs, we can expand very fast, but that expansion is problematic. It's not that we don't want it, we know that through NGOs the group will be sustained, but what we most wanted was to take theatre directly to the people at the grassroots, and that perhaps we are finding challenging now. In West Bengal we are okay, but in other states it can be very difficult.

Robyn: In the different states, is there someone in an overseeing role, similar to you, that is responsible for the work in their area?

Sanjoy: Yes, in Delhi they have a very good group and these people are responsible for organising the 'training for trainers' for the groups scattered in the neighbouring states that have come from activist movements. So in West Bengal, they are responsible for people in the west of India, and Delhi gives workshops to people in Uttar Pradesh, Rajasthan etc. That is how we wanted to move and actually it was moving quite successfully, but because of the tremendous crunch on funding, the process is getting slower.

Robyn: My next question is specific to the gang rape of a woman in Delhi that gained international news status. Did that have an impact on the work of JS? For example, during the protests, did JS do anything specifically related to that?

Sanjoy: The Centre for Social Studies (affiliated with the University of Jadavpur in Kolkata) will do research into JS's work around this issue as well as domestic violence, and this will reveal the truth.

We are very happy that the research will be conducted by one of the most reputable research institutes of the central government. So they will come and study and I think if you look at the cases of rape and killing (husbands killing their wives) in the last fifteen years in the whole central area of JS's operation in West Bengal, you will not find a single instance.

Now, people will come down the street with candles, it is a style that has come over from the West, and they will shout out loud, like anarchy, with no organisation, and after some time people will disappear. I don't think that this is the way to protest. When something happens, sometimes it is good. However, before something happens we have some duties, for example, the soap operas [e.g. *Jolnupur and Maa* – a Bengali soap opera, also look at national channel V] on Indian television are promoters of patriarchy. No organisation will address this because it is going to hit the corporate culture. If you see the advertisements, consumer market fundamentalism thinks that the relationship between a man and a woman is of a consumerist nature. Each one will consume the other, so the reflection of this idea is very much that in all advertisement. Nobody is talking about it. So the provocation is that men should see the woman as a consumer product and similarly a woman should see the man as a consumer product. This orientation is rapidly happening through media, advertisement, Bollywood movies. So naturally, the provocation is all around. I think in America the provocation is huge and when you are talking about the rape in Delhi, have they ever thought about how many thousand rapes there are in even one American city? The Delhi rape was publicised as if something happened in the world which is the rarest of the rare but which is actually very common and nobody is taking care of it. To take care of it you have to really attack market fundamentalism, which is primarily responsible for this kind of madness amongst the men. I cannot deny that a man can rape a woman and a woman cannot rape a man, it is very rare.

Patriarchy is there, so we have to include how patriarchy functions from school age when giving sex education. It is also important to make people understand from childhood that patriarchy is an inhuman value. Art should create a space to talk against patriarchy and create a war against patriarchy. We should try and find a mechanism to address this whole issue. There is no comprehensive, serious initiative for this. We are trying to figure out how to deal with it, a law cannot. There are thousands and thousands of laws in our country, which will never be implemented. When patriarchy is encouraged, when consumerism is encouraged so much, when people are deeply frustrated in their lives and they are finding no way to channel their frustration, we are creating a dream for everyone that 99 percent of people will fail to achieve their dream so your world can accommodate 1 percent. This 99 percent of frustrated, depressed people – where will they go? Sometimes this sort of happens. So society should include and accommodate people and help them to fulfil their dreams; what do you want to be, what do you want to do? You are restricted to one space, you have to be the most brilliant, and then you have a chance to survive in this society. That sort of society will always go towards violence. So fundamentally the social principle is wrong, fundamentally this logic of profit that is driving out the development principle is wrong. So we have to address that, and it is unfortunate that the people marching with candles and the artists are all demanding a law. It's taking a shortcut, it's not creating a long sustainable consistent move; people are always trying to find a shortcut. Even if there is a law, even if there is a death sentence, you cannot stop this problem.

Robyn: Do you think that the plays that you are performing such as *Golden Girl* and *The Brick Factory* is JS's way of combating this problem?

Sanjoy: That is the way to stop this criminal act in our society: let people think, together. This happens to the audience when an agricultural worker who is an oppressive husband finds himself on stage; sometimes he thinks, 'that's me on the stage', so he is the spectator of his own actions; 'this is how I act to my wife'. So by being the spectator of his own actions he finds an oppressive person: 'I am an agricultural worker, I am oppressed in the field but I am an oppressor in my home. He discovers that the human being inside him and the oppressive personality that he has contradict each other, and that's how you can make someone humanist. So we must talk about it, we must try to understand the problem, but we must question the social system.

Nowadays society only thinks of profits, no matter what values they are promoting. If you see the deodorant advertisement, it's patriarchy at an aggressive point. Nobody is opposing it, the government is passing laws on one hand to stop this but the same government is not censoring the advertisement that is continuously promoting this kind of criminal act. Before and after the

Delhi rape there were rapes happening in the villages all over but they are not in the capital of the country, therefore they didn't come to the surface of the media, nobody talked about it. Because it happened in Delhi and perhaps because she was a medical student so it came into the light. But it's not just Delhi, it's happening all around the country. I can tell you that I cannot remember a single incident in our operational area, in the last fifteen years where killing happened, where a rape or 'Eve-teasing'[1] happened. It used to happen, where a husband has killed his wife. Now, if there is a slightest tendency of 'Eve-teasing' by the young men, people take care of it.

Robyn: I'd like to ask you about women feeling able to intervene in Forum. For example, if a woman is suffering from domestic violence and there are people in the audience from her community, are there any negative repercussions from family members as a result of actively being involved with an intervention?

Sanjoy: No. However, as an outside agency, if you go to a village, if you do not have any rapport with the villagers, if the villagers do not see you as their friends . . .

Through JS, people are getting treated here [i.e. in our centre], they are using it as a shelter, we take them to hospital, we also see to it that if the villagers need a doctor, we take them to our doctor friends, we have a network with a lot of doctors who support JS for no cost, if there is a dispute about land, family, people call us to respond, to arbitrate. They feel that JS are their friends, if they have any problem with the administration they come to us, we take them to the government office, when they act against anything, we are always with them, on any issue we are always with them so they don't see us as the enemy. This gives us confidence to call the women on stage. They know that it is JS calling, so therefore our menfolk will not be unhappy. TO demands your attention, demands that you be part of the community. Theatre *for* the Oppressed doesn't have that, and in most cases Theatre *of* the Oppressed has turned into Theatre *for* the Oppressed. Very few people truly do Theatre *of* the Oppressed; the mark of those who do is that they believe that when you go to a village where you are just an outside agency, you should ensure that it is the people who speak.

When we go to a new village in a new area we always try to call men first to replace the female character: 'you have sisters, you have to arrange your daughter's marriage, if you were the daughter, if you were the mother, what would you do?' The moment the men come to replace the woman, that allows women to come on stage, the ice breaks. So then they come, and we hardly have any problem. I cannot even remember a single instance where we went to the women and had no interventions from them even in the new villages. In a very remote and distant village we went to perform *Golden Girl*, girls of fifteen, sixteen years, not the mother's age, as the mother is following the father-in-law, the grandchildren come on stage and do something. And that breaks the ice. Initially, you will get an intervention from the adolescent girl and then you go another time you will get an intervention from an adult woman and when you go another time it will get easier. The question we always get is whether we think about whether we will succeed or not; but we don't really consider that: it's not a matter of one time. One time you may not be successful, so it has to be consistent, if you are addressing an issue like patriarchy, there is no point going to the community once or twice. You have to make sure that your presence will be continuous, so people can identify you as their friends. This problem cannot be solved overnight, so it needs a long-term intervention.

Robyn: Have other companies used this JS model internationally?

Sanjoy: I think people have definitely been influenced by it. It has inspired a lot of groups who try their best to be present in a community, to be friends with the community. In Germany, in France, in Spain, in England, there are groups that are really inspired. But in the West there are some specific difficulties, here we have other specific difficulties, so naturally, I can't expect the model of JS to be totally replicated in Europe. But more or less the ideas and the philosophies can be implemented, trying to get connected with a community where they can go frequently. In France, a group go to an immigrant community and the unemployed and work with them regularly [Ed: T'OP! Théâtre, Lille].

Robyn: Some of your teams now are all female, does that have an impact on how people interact with them?

Sanjoy: Women acting as men definitely has an impact, to prepare a community to that level took at least ten years [going from all-male to all-female performances]. In our area, women are leaders, women are in power not only in relation to their own issues but also issues such as education, alcoholism, security. The women's voice is something very prominent in all the JS areas.

Robyn: Do you think it's less intimidating for a woman who has never intervened before to go onstage?

Sanjoy: Yes, maybe it has helped other women, as they are all women on stage. However, we don't really believe that it is important because if you address the problem and you are serious about it, then the women will come on stage anyway – that is what we believe.

But also there is a practical purpose because sometimes men have to migrate for months, and this seasonal migration affects the mixed teams. Therefore, we decided for practical purposes, because the women in our area do not migrate, we have women's teams to continue the plays. That was the point of view of how we started our female teams but now it is a political statement to others.

Robyn: How did the men react to it at first?

Sanjoy: The first women to perform were actually the sisters and wives of our male performers; we started with their families. Naturally they enjoyed the support from their house. This has inspired women and men so much that now it has become a culture in that area to have all-women's plays, not only JS plays but plays with both men's and women's characters, and when men are not present they perform the play themselves; we have made it a fashion.

In Theatre of the Oppressed, if it is truly understood, there should be no conflict between men and women, because there is dialogue and democracy. The idea that it significantly affects the practice of TO depending on whether there is a woman or a man as the joker is misguided. The essential thing is that the role of the joker is to facilitate dialogue and allow people to get connected.

The second thing is, from my experience of doing TO for such a long span of time, over a quarter of a century, I think that women are more interested in this particular theatre than men. In my workshop whenever we go to the West, more than 70 percent of participants are women. And do they have no potential to be jokers? How can you underestimate them? Because Boal was a man dominating this or maybe in JS I have directed, maybe Julian Boal and some others are men in the TO scene but that doesn't mean there are no women. There are brilliant women jokers, all around, they just haven't caught the fame. Getting fame is a very different kind of ball game, I know women jokers always interested in putting things on social media and publicising their work and reshaping their work in a way that they can get attention from the system and government. There are a lot of women jokers – mostly TO is dominated by the women.

For me, jokering is not an important task, just like refereeing in football. Actually, twenty-two people are playing the sport and they are the ones who score the goals. The role of the joker is to follow the argument of the spect-actors and oppressive characters. But actually whether a Forum theatre will be a success or not depends completely on the actors, particularly the oppressive character. If he is tricky, clever and very clear about his ideology, he will make things very hard for the spect-actors and therefore the debate will proceed further and further, and then the actors will join. Sometimes they will have to decide when they want to support, maybe the protagonist is failing, they have to add some energy to it; this is the decision of the actors. People often think that the joker is all-important. Sometimes the jokers want to be so visible that I feel very angry about it, they are jumping on the stage and moving from here to here. It's important to be *in*visible. Just because mainly the jokers are men doesn't mean that the women's roles should be undermined because the actors are mostly women and they make Forum theatre successful. If an oppressive character cannot problematise, if they don't perform well, then even a good joker will fail. The joker is empowered by the actors.

Robyn: Being an oppressor is emotionally draining: when you have that experience of being that person on stage, especially if you are drawing from your own experience, it can be quite a difficult thing to do.

Sanjoy: It is the job of the actors to understand that their role is to take people to the world of rationality; they have to have this in mind. But spect-actors sometimes may get emotional – that we should allow. Then we should tell people that we want to go *towards* the rational. It's not the fault of the spect-actors – you cannot say 'why are you doing this?' if she or he has suffered from this. At the same time, the joker's responsibility is to tell people that the same woman can act differently. In our theatre, we have seen that the oppressed woman, who has suffered from the oppression of her husband, can play a very strong oppressor. Because she has experienced the oppression, she knows how the oppressor acts, that's true.

A scene from *Where We Stand*

Note

1 An Indian euphemism for sexual harassment (Ed.).

Interview 3
Interview with Sanjoy Ganguly, 27 December 2013

Conducted by Clément Poutot

Clément: How does Jana Sanskriti aim to solve traditional problems in the villages, such as patriarchy?
Sanjoy: I'm struggling to answer your question. For example, when you ask a question on tradition, then we must ask: 'what is tradition?' Tradition is something that has been happening for a long time. What do we mean by a long time? For example, when you are addressing domestic violence, that is not always a product of tradition. In many ways, capitalism plays a role. You see, patriarchy has existed during feudalism, capitalism and modern capitalism. So that means that sometimes some cultural values continue even though there are noticeable radical changes in the economy. If you look at so-called socialist economies like China, Soviet Russia, for example, they went through a radically different economy for a substantial period of time but patriarchy was there. Domestic violence was there. The vindictive attitude towards women by men was there. That means the system, for its own sustenance, doesn't rely only on economy, it constructs the cultural values, and this sometimes means keeping values that have been in practice for ages. So if you identify an existing patriarchal relationship between men and women, can you call it traditional? Because it existed at every phase of the economy and it still exists. You can see that there are rapes and aggression against women happening all over the world. Patriarchy in the Western sense is seen only from a gender perspective. But patriarchy is also manifested in authoritarianism, dictatorship and centralisation. The world has witnessed women patriarchs like Margaret Thatcher, Indira Gandhi, and many others. So patriarchy has many other dimensions besides gender.
Clément: So you think that cultural problems are caused by economic and political systems?

Sanjoy: Now, for example, in Delhi a girl was raped, and civil society protested. Why did they protest? They thought it was an aggression, a brutality. They demanded a law that could prevent this sort of brutal action. But what is a law? For example, in a distant district in South Bengal, there is a community that works in the stone crushing industry, they make big stones into stone chips. In those factories the women that work there regularly get raped by their contractors. It is an open secret: if the contractor calls a woman worker to his room alone, the women have to go. So now, there is a law. But if a woman, to protect herself from aggression, goes to the law, she would lose her job. So even though there is a law, she cannot make use of it. She wants to be free from poverty, free from unemployment: to have economic security. In this case the oppression against women cannot be in isolation from the issue of unemployment and poverty. The law is not enough.

Clément: So would you argue that capitalism is the main source, or are there others?

Sanjoy: So patriarchy in isolation from aggressive capitalistic development cannot address the entire scale, the whole source of the problem. There are causes responsible for strengthening patriarchy as an effect. It is predominantly connected to the market economy. We have television series here and there. We see the shameless promotion of patriarchy and male snobbism. The viewers swallow them regularly. The advertisement of various products glorifies and praises male snobbism and projects the idea that men and women should see themselves as consumer products – relationships should be based on sexual consumption. Sex is a consumer item, a business product in our film industries. In the modern market, sex is a product that is sellable. Sex is not a dimension of love. Do you still think that in addressing patriarchy we are addressing only Indian tradition? Most gynaecological diseases grow to a very dangerous level because women don't think their health is important. Most women are suffering from malnutrition and anaemia in India today. Why are nearly 80 percent of women anaemic? This is a modern picture, not traditional.

Clément: So you think we need to look at the modern system to solve these problems?

Sanjoy: The problem inside the development paradigm is not being addressed. And we are seeing it in isolation and branding it as a traditional practice continuing for ages, which is perhaps not the right conclusion.

It is not a question of tradition. It is a question of a system sustaining itself by deliberately trying to make sure that some values remain present in society. So when we're going to perform a play on oppression of women, for example, we're not trying to change a tradition. We are actually trying to find the irrationalities in the modern system and in the modern market economy. The whole question of unequal power relations between men and women has always been nourished by the system imposed upon people. This is what we have to understand, we should not only focus on the effect; we should also try to understand the causes behind an effect. And that is principally the role of Theatre of the Oppressed. So through our plays about oppression of women, we are talking about domestic violence in order to understand how patriarchy is responsible for allowing domestic violence to work as an ideology in our psyche.

Clément: So you want to expose audiences to this?

Sanjoy: That is why we do our performances: it is not to find a magic solution in a Forum theatre session. That is one dimension. But the practice of Forum theatre should take actors and spectators to the better sociological understanding of the problem. It's not a question of changing tradition, it's a question of establishing rationality, which is always modern. What we are saying today will be tradition after a hundred years. There have been always two streams in all ages. One acts for the existing situation and another acts for transformation or for change in society. So examining tradition to find irrationalities and rationalities in it is important. The same thing is important for modernity. It is not primarily a question of choosing between tradition or modernity, we need to find the rationality in both.

Clément: So what is traditional, in your view?

Sanjoy: If you look at tradition objectively, you can see the strong presence of patriarchy and its parallel: the fight against patriarchy. The struggle against an orthodox dogmatic system by the then progressive forces has made us advanced in thinking. In our social system, early marriage at the age of three years to six years was tradition, but also the fight against this system was part of our tradition. Now you see that the caste system is a source of sustenance for many political parties in India. Instead of abolishing caste, they are re-imposing the caste system. They have corporate sponsors. Who gives them so much money to run such parties? Leaders in those parties are filthy rich. The modern capitalistic system perpetuates the concept of caste in order to divide communities, and then funds NGOs under their control to fight the caste system; it promotes communalism for its own ends [Ed: in Indian usage, communalism means intercommunal antagonism] and funds its chosen NGOs to run a peace project. It's like asking a burglar to steal and at the same time asking the house owner to be cautious. Religious fundamentalism and the caste system are more a construct of the state than of religion. The controlling forces of capital have deliberately perpetuated some divisive social factors in order to ensure that there is no united resistance.

In claiming to be modern and advanced, this position encourages a simplistic view of tradition for its own ends; so we do not examine that tradition. So how can society progress if it doesn't learn from its past?

Clément: How do you believe society can progress?

Sanjoy: The objective way is to see how conflict existed in terms of progressive and conservative positions in the past and how society advanced in a humane direction. So our strategy is to reexamine tradition and reexamine what we had. Of course, some things disappear in this conflict and some remain. That is the journey towards humanism. But according to the modern logic of profit, every citizen has to accept a single definition of development, one definition of art and culture; the priests of modern capital claim that there is no alternative.

Human rights is a space where people intellectually grow and discover their ability to think and have the rationale to examine society. When you stop people from developing such understanding, you are violating human rights and stopping people developing an understanding by creating a culture of monologue. It's a didactic way of approaching development. That happened in the Soviet bloc and it is happening in capitalism. So by abandoning socialism we gained nothing – we are still not free because we are thinking through the frame prescribed by the modern system.

Clément: So how does Jana Sanskriti work to solve this problem?

Sanjoy: The aim of Theatre of the Oppressed to me is to develop an objectivity which will help people to discover irrationality in tradition and in the modern exploitative system. Theatre of the Oppressed believes in rationalising society from the perspective of the oppressed.

Clément: And you think it's possible to create a rational analysis of tradition?

Sanjoy: Of course. Particularly on the question of patriarchy. Obviously it is an age-old problem, so you can call it a tradition, but a tradition of what? A tradition of feudalism? A tradition of modern capitalism? We must try to understand why some tradition is still continuing today. One important thing is that we should evaluate the conflict between inhuman and human values in tradition considering the economic, political and social contexts of those days. Often when we judge leading personalities from the old days we make this mistake and we forget to evaluate our own actions in the present. I think to address an oppression, you need to be neither traditional nor modern. We have to create a space where people will be thinking rationally and thus will become rational.

Clément: So can you give a concrete example of modern systems being the cause of what some interpret as a traditional problem that compromises human rights?

Sanjoy: Recently Jana Sanskriti and a group of very pro-people medical doctors have come together to demand universal health care. In this movement, Jana Sanskriti is responsible for launching a theatrical campaign to talk about the issue and to understand the villager's perspective on universal health care. My doctor friends who went to work in the villages said they could only deliver modern medicine; that was what they knew about. Medicine and politics have both abandoned tradition. This is a kind of fundamentalism we always cultivate in our political practices. Doubtless facilities for doing research into traditional medicine have been lacking. There are few standardised methods of preparing it, no consistency about dosage, no analysis of potentially harmful ingredients. But research also did not take place because the drug industry lobby wanted to wipe out traditional knowledge and create a knowledge which would support their 'logic of profit'. That's how they do it. Now some multinational corporations have started marketing medicines made from herbs and plants – they have also patented some of them. Those medicines are very expensive. Does that not mean traditional knowledge on medicine is being appropriated by corporate capital? Knowledge is becoming centralised from a poor and marginal population to corporate interests. We were trying to convince the doctors that there is traditional knowledge but that some people who have the knowledge will get old, and they will die. And with their death, that knowledge will disappear. So our only knowledge, our only option will be provided by the modern system. That is didactic in nature. So now our task should be to gather the knowledge scattered all around and examine it, and apply some science to it and protect it and give it back to the people so that they don't have to depend only on modern medicines – so that tradition and modern practice can come together. We have to be rational and see what interesting scientific elements are there in the tradition and what is in modern thinking, so we can make a combination.

Clément: And you think that the logic of profit is affecting industries other than the health system?

Sanjoy: In agriculture we had thousands of varieties of seeds, but they have disappeared. What exists are the seeds given by the corporations. So now they're coming up for a second green revolution, which is also designed by the corporations but is strongly rejected in Europe. It is based on the logic of profit. The first green revolution in India abandoned traditional farming practices. The companies stole the independence of the farming community. The land now has become non-fertile, the use of pesticides and insecticides has destroyed the bacteria good for farming, has killed a lot of friendly insects, has badly affected biodiversity and human health. Is this modern or irrationalism? It is an irrationalism based on the logic of profit.

Clément: So how can theatre solve this problem?

Sanjoy: Theatre of the Oppressed essentially is a dialectic style of thinking. So we have to be careful about branding anything as either tradition or as modern. We have to find where rationality exists: that's the search, that's the exercise. It is not a problem-solving solution. If you go with the objective of stopping domestic violence, that means that you are giving advice. You will not be able to discover the other dimensions in this whole game. If you discover the other dimensions in this whole game, automatically this immediate violence will be addressed by the people with an overall understanding of how this happens, what the genesis is. And accordingly they will act. It is a rational act. And Theatre of the Oppressed is intended to ensure this rational act. That is why it is anti-system.

But if theatre is not taking people into the world of rationality, it is just trying to address an immediate problem and an immediate solution, then it functions as a useful tool for the system, which receives funding, promotion and patronisation. We have to see the deficiencies in our practices. The most important thing is to develop Theatre of the Oppressed as a space for rational thinking based on liberation and not based on what the market demands. That is to really understand the way in which Boal assimilated Marx.

Clément: In the last festival, when we were in the Sunderbans, we had a performance where Stephen performed along with a girl. It was the story of an African girl who married a man from the West and the family rejected the African girl – do you remember it? Then the African girl went to a school to be Western. In the forum, most spect-actors did not like this uniformisation, they pleaded for the existence of the diversified culture. Can you remember? This is rational thinking, this is something beyond tradition and modernity.

Sanjoy: We have a caste system in India. It's an age-old problem. Who's reinforcing the caste system today in India: is it a religious construct or a political construct? It's political: you can see there are political leaders who would not survive without the existence of the caste system. Those political parties are funded by the corporations. The prime ministerial candidate projected by a political party is a communal figure. He slaughtered a lot of Muslims in 2002 in Gujarat. This guy is the darling of the Indian capitalists [Ed: current Indian Prime Minister Narendra Modi].

Therefore the caste system and communalism today is a state-sponsored political construct, as well as being part of a culture of irrationality nourished by today's politics and social system. In the Indian epics there are several instances where Brahmanism was defined and the hierarchy of caste was invoked. But there were also instances which did not support this interpretation.

Clément: Do you think this problem is specific to India?

Sanjoy: You can see racism present as another form of caste in Europe. Who constructs racism? Who is becoming racist in the modern system? Why do we see racism in Europe? This is not a result of tradition, it is modernity. It is economy, the logic of profit, it is imperialism. It demands the creation of the Taliban in Afghanistan and demands civil wars between ethnic groups in Afghanistan. So by branding religious groups in Afghanistan as traditional, superpowers are actually using this concept, they are reinforcing, nourishing and developing it because it serves their interests. So that is why instead of branding something as traditional, people should re-examine it – is it traditional anymore? Is it the tradition of the people? Or is it just the tradition of the coloniser to keep the divisive forces alive?

People want to be united, they fought against their oppressors, they were united, but after their struggle was over again, they got divided. For example, there are factories where workers fight together for their wages and benefits. But the same workers, when they leave the factory, they belong to Hindu parties, and Muslim parties and they are casteists and separatists.

Clément: So what do you think is most important in solving this hypocrisy?

Sanjoy: Why do trade unionists not address this in their political practice? When they are working for the workers, fighting for their wages, this cannot be called a collective action. The action is based on self-interest. And ultimately it gives you a temporary win – my wages will increase. But my life will not be changed because in a way we will be supporting the divisive values. So we have to address this lack in our political practice. So when you are doing Theatre of the Oppressed you have to make sure that these factors can be understood by the workers. Development of this understanding is Theatre of the Oppressed to me, and unfortunately this is absent in many spheres. We have been fed some terms, some terminology, some model of tradition and modernity and we have completely succumbed to it. But we are now beginning to look beyond the bland assertions. So if when you are addressing the caste system you begin to think about how it originated and how it was nourished and why and how it still exists in the capitalistic system even today, this understanding is very important.

Clément: Can you give any other examples of contemporary problems caused by irrational thought?

Sanjoy: Why does every Indian have to be Western? Who has constructed this ideology for the people? From very ancient times in India, lots of people from various races and religions came and settled here. People here say we do not tolerate other religions under compulsion, we accept all religions. So when people say we accept other religions, I think that is a modern statement. I think that if people from India and the world could have absorbed the rationality in this traditional modern statement about race and religion, we could have made the world free from communalism, racism and castes. But it still exists. Why does this exist? Why did it not change with the change in economic structure? What we need is to nourish our rationality, which existed in the past and exists in the present. So we have to find out how we can make ourselves more rational.

Clément: Do you believe all people have the facility to think rationally?

Sanjoy: In the last festival some participants of my workshop made a play on racism. They portrayed a scene where a family from the West does not accept the fact that the boy in their family loves an African girl. We conducted a Forum theatre session on that scene. We noticed that people by and large do not want this racist view to grow. The Forum session to a large extent tried to break the conditioning of the racist mind. This kind of matter demands consistent and continuous intervention. One Forum show is just nothing and meaningless. On the surface there sometimes appear to be large differences between Indian and Western culture, yet all the spectators, from India or abroad, could recognise the situation. There was a common rationality. So even though there are cultural differences, it is important to cultivate an openness, so that Europeans can accept the rational element of the Indian or African culture and Indians can accept the rational element in Western culture. Therefore we should widen the space, and discuss all of this. That's why when Jessica, the American actress and drama teacher, asked if villagers in our area would be able to respond to this example of Western experience, I replied, 'Why don't you give it a try? They might not have the right direction of thinking, but they will be thinking and then will try to develop an understanding.'

Now in fact the interventions which came in the Forum were very culture specific, because we all think in terms of 'we' and 'they'. This is the result of the idea of nation state. A worker in England won't consider the interest of a worker in India. Even 'workers of the world unite', the very slogan, has no value today. Globalisation of capital does not preach one world, one humanity. What it wants is that everyone in this world should follow one development model, one cultural value, one single perspective of life. There will be no space for diversity in thinking. So the politics of globalisation is to destroy plurality and it is important in TO to resist this. How can we cultivate unity if diversity does not exist?

Clément: In your plays, you say you have one topic, and behind this you have the structure of the problem. Can you develop this point?

Sanjoy: I always make the statement that process is as important as the product. You have seen me working in Lille recently. Why did I give so much stress to the process of making a play there? I was not dictating anything, I was letting everyone think critically so that the actors have critical thinking before they go into a performance. If they have this critical thinking in mind, they'll make each intervention problematic and critical. And this problematisation will provoke people to be more critical. If you make it too simple, people will not be critical. So it is the job of the actors and the jokers to understand it critically. You cannot add all the complexities and criticalities in each character but as a character you should know you are critical and complex and a combination of many tendencies. That is why you have seen me doing analytical images on characters. And when the spect-actors come onto the stage, the dialogue between spect-actor and the oppressor character becomes very important. That problematises the situation and makes people critical. And taking people into this critical world is what is called Forum theatre.

Clément: My next question is how is it possible to create a complex character if you don't know the character you're creating? Is it a difficulty if the actor hasn't experienced it yet? In the play about Monsanto, for example.

Sanjoy: It is difficult: it's a new experiment. But you need to ask these questions of the people. Because the government came up with a policy and people don't have the knowledge to question this policy. That's not good, that's what we're trying to discuss. But the discussion of this problem is very difficult, because it is so specialised that not everyone can understand easily: the farmers have better knowledge of farming, for example, but even then they accepted the idea of the green revolution, which introduced terminator seeds, pesticides, chemical fertiliser. In the process a number of varieties of seeds have disappeared, the land is destroyed to a large extent. Now Monsanto is trying to introduce genetically modified organisms, they are planning to encourage cash crops, their partners Walmart and Metro Cash and Carry will be marketing them. So Indian farmers will produce crops for the middle class of 'developed' nations and 'developed' nations will export the food we will require. A section of scientists and political leaders are advocating this new agriculture. More than 77 percent of the Indian population lives on farming, so establishing control over agriculture means taking away food sovereignty. But to understand the problem we invited noted agricultural scientists, physicists, medical doctors, economists. They helped us in scripting a play questioning the introduction of GM crops by Monsanto.

But still we think our training isn't sufficient. So we need to give more time for the process: we need to be better trained. For example, if we're going to talk about health systems, one aspect is the provision of treatment: we don't know all that the doctors know. That is why we invite the doctors. I take doctors from Kolkata to the villages. And they conduct the sessions and make people understand what is generic and what is branded. Why do we want generic medicines? So this understanding is very important before you go to construct a play: the help of the doctors is part of the play-making process.

But returning to your point about actors understanding their roles, that is what is often missing in the play-making process. We talk about problems we ourselves do not know very well. People don't pay much attention to the process. You need to conduct workshops with the purpose of understanding the problem meticulously. If an actor playing the oppressor character does not know the ideology, the arguments of the oppressor in real life, he won't be able to portray the oppressor to the spectator. Improper portrayal of the oppressor character can be misleading and in that case the Forum session can't help spect-actors to debate and dialogue on the oppression shown in the play.

That is where I think Forum theatre is lacking. We have failed to discover the scope it can offer. We have made it very limited. We have to understand the wider scope in the whole practice of Forum theatre and Theatre of the Oppressed in general.

At the end let me tell you that our work is to find rationality in tradition and in modernity, rationality from a democratic and human point of view and not from the point of view of the profit-making economy.

A scene from *Unnayan* (Development)

Interview 4
Interview with Sanjoy Ganguly, November 2014, Vienna

Conducted by Joschka Köck

Joschka: So the first question would be: How were your experiences with volunteers and interns from Europe with Jana Sankriti? How were they helpful? What were the challenges? Did you establish a long-term connection and what was the impact of these people on the movement Jana Sanskriti?

Sanjoy: See, Jana Sanskriti evolved as a space for many people from Europe to come and meet, get to know each other, get connected. Sometimes, often, you see that, for example in Barcelona, there are five TO groups practising but they don't know each other, but when they are coming to Jana Sankriti, they can come to know: 'You are from Barcelona, oh yes, I am Pitteresa, oh I'm Patatam.' So they are building connectedness. Jana Sanskriti is acting as a space where people get connected. So that is why the idea of creating an international centre in Jana Sanskriti is in our mind, so that more people can come and get connected. And in this connection of course we learn. I can't say there were not one or two strange occurrences where we see that people go there for fun or they are dogmatic in many ways, but mostly, people find it very useful, and we also find it very useful. From the methodological point of view we learn from people, from the ideas point of view we argue, so therefore we deconstruct our ideas, this helps us. And also in the process, Jana Sanskriti has developed a wider range of friends from all across the world. You know, so we feel very fortunate that we are not alone. We don't see ourselves as a movement in India. We feel this connection, that we are connected with the world, because a lot of people come and share their experiences and we learn from each other. Except for one or two strange cases most of them are helpful.

This is another important aspect: Even though Jana Sanskriti is known as a Theatre of the Oppressed group, it thinks that Theatre of the Oppressed is being developed, is being recreated, restructured by many people in the world. So thoughts are playing. And you know, I heard this from a person in Varanasi. He said: 'Thoughts evolve when people mingle.' So because a lot of these people are trying to go beyond what it is there today, this thought mingles and strengthens your thoughts, raises questions, confusions, convictions. So JS also thinks that Theatre of the Oppressed needs to take a journey. It needs to be evolved, you know. And because it needs to be evolved we should have negotiation with other schools of thought as well. It is not only TO. So a lot of people from other schools of theatre should also go to JS.

Joschka: And schools of politics, too?

Sanjoy: Schools of politics also, it's true, because the negotiation is very important. To climb to the top of the hill there are many paths; that you have to accept. So if the goal is to humanise human beings or human society, then the paths can be different, but we should have a negotiation. Because we all are trying to get to the same place. So there is a flexibility that JS offers for many people. Therefore people feel like coming, getting connected and we also learn from them and they also learn from us.

Joschka: So do you feel that this negotiation process is happening on equal terms? Or do you think there is a North-South power relation that also affects the work that Jana Sanskriti is doing in the international network or community of TO or other schools of thought?

Sanjoy: I can't, I cannot totally. It is difficult for me to answer because you are also right in some way. Because Jana Sanskriti is today seen as a point of reference. So that sort of 'privileged people going to help' model, these sort of things don't much happen in Jana Sanskriti. Because it already has a very wide reputation and it has its record of work. So we don't experience it. But this sometimes happens in this workshop culture. People from North go to South to deliver a workshop, you know for a project or things like that. And it doesn't really help the Theatre of the Oppressed. It's not helping. It is creating a kind of hierarchy. So there, it is true that in some spaces I find in the so-called harder world, this hierarchy is big. So therefore it is in no way strengthening the Theatre of the Oppressed movement. Rather it is breaking the community. Theatre of the Oppressed is finding it difficult to evolve as a community. But in JS fortunately we don't experience this, because people regard our group from a very high, respectable point of view. But I know your question is right.

Joschka: Maybe also in regard to the workshop process we developed like yesterday and the day before yesterday, I think that a lot of power relations also go into the creation of the script, if we develop the script and script the play, then who is heard in developing the script is also a power question, so maybe how do you avoid it? How can you try to overcome this challenge of TO?

Sanjoy: When you are working in a group, sometimes I find one person is very active, taking more space. But TO is a method that prevents him from taking a larger space. Sometimes it doesn't work, but if you keep doing it, then it will suddenly work. If I ask you to go again and again to go restructure the structure, the structure, the structure, then one man cannot have this space all on his own.

But there will be some specialisation in a group. Maybe someone is good at structuring, and someone is good at going deeper into the analysis. So it is a collective work. Each of them will contribute from their own expertise. Not everyone is good at mathematics. Someone can be good at mathematics, someone can be good at Bengali. Someone can be good at organisation, someone can be good at presenting the group, someone can be good at leading the workshop. We have to learn how to see it as collectively informed. We may have our own expertise, we may have our own area of choice. But they need to be connected. And that's the thing we need to learn. JS has evolved such a big group because we knew that we have our own area of choice, but each of us is complementing the whole.

Joschka: So one of the last questions would be: What advice would you give us to create a TO movement in Vienna, as young TO practitioners?

Sanjoy: I cannot advise you, but from my experience I can tell you that you need four things. One is patience. Patience to hear others and patience to understand that your work cannot give you an immediate result. So you need to have patience, you need to have tolerance, respect and most importantly love. You have to cultivate love. And that's the area, if you love, then your dogma will always find it difficult to act. So basically we want to, we need to develop our own paradigm. What I am saying, that if you are a Gandhian, you see things from the Gandhian point of view. If you are a Marxist, you observe something from the Marxist point of view. So your observation is not a true observation, because you are watching it from a frame. So unless you go outside the frame, you cannot truly observe.

So I would request you to truly observe and truly listen to others. When you are listening you have to empty yourselves first. So that's the paradigm.

So developing this paradigm means you are leaving dogma behind; and in this case it is not only a theory that I have to empty

	myself, to listen to this, I have to go beyond the frame, it's not a theory it is a realisation. And the realisation comes from the love.
Joschka:	You know what we are experiencing, I think, in Vienna is this huge anonymity of people. They are not talking to each other, there is no connectivity between people in the city, so I would like to have some advice how to work against this.
Sanjoy:	But you know, you have to create an example. People should see that you are consistently acting with their differences. And you are looking at differences as your strengths, not as hard for you. If you can see this, if you can succeed in accepting difference as strengths (and there are various paths to that), then I think you will be able to connect yourselves. And if you can give an example for the people, you know? Don't split away because you were not satisfied. Because your position was not accepted. So if you leave behind this culture of seeing difference from a negative point of view, then you will be able to put forward an example to the people. This one example can create a hundred more examples. So it is a process. It's not a product. You have to continuously be part of the process. You never know when you will see the effects. You may think that, well, we have been doing Forum theatre for so many years, being connected to each other as a group, as a collective. We have advanced a lot, but even then I can't see the effect. The effect cannot be seen through the eyes, you know, the effect can happen later.
Joschka:	You can feel it maybe.
Sanjoy:	You can feel it.
Joschka:	Yeah, thank you.
Sanjoy:	Thank you.

Interview 5
Interview with Sanjoy Ganguly on Vivekananda, January 2014

Conducted by Clément Poutot

Clément: How did Vivekananda come to influence your theatre?
Sanjoy: My understanding of Vivekananda started much later than my work in theatre, actually. He is known superficially to every Indian. As an Indian I now know him, but previously I really didn't know Vivekananda properly. The orientation of the Communist Party tended to dispose us to ignore ideas which were present in Indian philosophy, it made us feel that all progressive thought originated in the West. That was not just to do with economics but more a cultural bias, it was a kind of Westernisation of thought. So I didn't have a critical and objective view of what Vivekananda thought before I went to the village. What I took with me to the village was my experience in the Party where the opinions of the people do not matter, where a kind of religiosity is practised. The Party created leader Gods, these gods are both international and national; and there is a clean visible line between intellectuals and non-intellectuals. So I experienced the rule of elitism inside the Party, the culture of Vanguards. 'We will lead'; 'the people are not intellectuals': only this privileged section of the middle class which has been exposed to these ideas in education can construct the revolutionary theories. That sort of belief I saw inside the Party. So, when I didn't experience any space for independent thought, when I didn't experience the recognition of the intellectual ability of the people living in the margin, I left the Party and went to the village. And in the village when I started experiencing how people think if they are given the opportunity, I realised that what I was taught inside the Party was completely wrong. So I had to deal with it. At that point of time I was interested in Vivekananda because he was the only thinker I had come across who recognised the intellectual faculty of the people. Then I started reading him.

One more reason why Vivekananda came to my attention needs to be mentioned. When I started watching folk art, traditional art, I realised that our traditional art wanted to make people social critics. Many stories from the Indian epics [Ed: *Mahabharata, Ramayana*] and stories from the *Puranas* used to be played in the folk theatre and in other traditional art forms. Most of them were very controversial. The epic writers portrayed the characters of gods in a very controversial way without any fear. But inside the Party no big leader can be controversial to the rank and file. We are not permitted to see any controversy about leaders, they are given cult status. If you are a Stalinist, Stalin is god. If you are a Trotskyist, Trotsky is god. There is no controversy about them. But in the epics we find a different and opposite trend. That attracted me, so that inspired me to read the epics. And slowly slowly I started feeling interested in reading epics and philosophy which originated in India. I began to understand that epics are the collective creation of the people, and that was why the epics were the dominant subject in traditional theatre. Then Vivekananda came into my life. I read his phenomenal book *Prachya Paschattya*, which means 'East and West'.

Vivekananda from the beginning was very striking to me because he didn't always talk like a spiritual man, a conventional spiritual person. He went much beyond institutional religion, he spoke like a revolutionary politician. And to me Vivekananda is the first person in India who talked about socialism. He spoke about it in 1897. But perhaps he understood the limitation of the existing concept of socialism. That is why he said socialism is not a foolproof system, but half a loaf is better than having no loaf at all. That is where Vivekananda was not acceptable to the Communist Party here, because Indian communists used to hold up an umbrella over their head if it was raining in Moscow. They didn't have time to read what Vivekananda said. For me he was a combination of rational tradition and rational modernity (given the fact that not everything is rational in tradition and in modernity). He was not conservative, he was very scientific. He didn't believe in doctrine, he believed in philosophy. His way of looking at people was different. He said: people need information. Information is centralised. So give them information and they will examine this information in the light of their experience, from the information they have already acquired from experience. According to Vivekananda the information people already have from experience and the information they acquire through any medium act against each other constructively. This constructive conflict generates new theory.

So he came up with the example of Newton. Newton noticed an apple falling from the tree. This was information given by nature. He had already some more information in his head. With this information he started questioning the phenomenon he had observed. And he finally discovered the law of gravitation. But the law of gravitation was already there. Essentially, people discover what is already there. But they discover by acquiring information and challenging both what they have acquired and what they knew previously: this conflict of information creates knowledge. So what they need is information. Information given and information already possessed constructs knowledge through a dynamic process of 'constructive conflict' and complementarity.

That is how he recognised the intellectual faculty of all human beings and wanted to create a democratic form of politics which provokes people to think. He actually preached a democratised politics. He was in favour of *'Politics of the Oppressed'* and not of *'Politics for the Oppressed'*. The so-called dictatorship of the proletariat was also a dictatorship over the proletariat by the Party. Something like this may have been necessary in the beginning and was followed by what was perhaps conceived of as a community of benevolent kings. But unfortunately it established a monologic and oppressive structure. People should have been given more space to think and articulate their views. One single view cannot dominate a society. Modern capitalism is now once again imposing a single view on us and that is oppressive. Margaret Thatcher clearly expressed the sociology of modern capital with her TINA [There Is No Alternative]. What we find today is authoritarianism disguised as democracy, pollution in democracy is a global phenomenon. If capitalism never encouraged any society except capitalism, why is this? Because capitalism also does not believe in diversity. That is the reason it adopted the means of religiosity and violence to destroy socialism. Socialism on the other hand did not mature because it had the same problem, millions of people in the former USSR were killed in the name of "socialism"! Vivekananda basically wanted the proletariat to think, which is echoed in what Boal said, and in what Forum Theatre wants to achieve. Vivekananda didn't have the dramaturgy, he was not a theatre person, but he had the theory on which the dramaturgy of Theatre of the Oppressed is founded.

Vivekananda to me was very important. He was talking about a new kind of democracy, true democracy and dialogue. And that is the reason why he did appreciate the reforms of the nineteenth century and offered a very important critique from the perspective of participation and democratisation of politics. Undoubtedly the reform in the nineteenth century Bengal was led by the educated elite and middle class, they determined the issues, they did not take into account the voices of the majority living in the villages, living in the margin. After the 1857 mutiny in India, the British realised that arms were not enough to rule India. So they decided to use culture as armaments. They tactically positioned their culture as superior to our culture, that's how they developed an inferiority among Indians, so that Indians would accept British rule. The British education system started to develop an Indo-English section which would be Indian by birth and blood but English at heart; however by default it also led to the development of a section of people who were Indian by heart and had a wider vision. History has other examples of such situations where the coloniser does something to achieve their own narrow goal but thereby also serves the colonised in some ways. Marx has called this an 'unwilling contribution'. In this case, people emerged from the education system with a desire to reform their society, because the society at that time was very conservative, superstitious, and beset by an ugly fundamentalism in religion. It was partly natural, when a race does not have a political platform to voice their anger against cultural imposition and cannot act against political and economic slavery imposed by a colonial power, they choose to be additionally attached to their own culture, no matter how limited it is. The fact however was that the reform was defined from the perspective of the British. It was like cleaning the society with the eyes of the English. The perspective of the majority located in the margin was not even considered. Most reformers did not question the sociology of hunger, famine and epidemic that were part of the lives of the people in the margin killing millions. Vivekananda from the beginning was a critic of this top-down approach. He thought that legislation without rational participation is not enough, though he had a respect for the movement of reform at his time.

I experienced how the Party looks at people, their patronising approach, their disempowering political practice, a practice of 'follow me' culture, a religiosity in other words. So between the activism of the reformers of the nineteenth century and Vivekananda,

I prefer Vivekananda. To me he seems still more a contemporary than a figure of the nineteenth century.

Clément: Last time, we spoke about the sentence of Vivekanada: 'education is the manifestation of perfection already in man . . .'

Sanjoy: That is the most striking sentence which changed my way of looking at people. The understanding of that sentence helped me to learn from those who are educated but 'illiterate' in the normal sense, it brought me close to the wisdom and philosophical teaching of the 'illiterate' people.

Then I found Vivekananda said, in his writing 'people who love god are religious, people who love man are god'. Basically his concept of God is very different from that of conventional religion. His god doesn't exist in the sky. His god exists in every human being. This is the clearest definition of de-classing. That's how he wants to establish equality in society. If everyone is potentially God, then how can there be division, discrimination, separation, class? I call this a spiritual dimension in his political thought, but you can call it anything. But his concept of equality goes beyond mere economic equality. Even if there is economic equality we can have differences. If you are an intellectual, if you are an engineer, if you are a doctor, will you be able to overcome your egoic sense of yourself as a part of the intelligentsia? You tend not to think of a worker as having the same status as a doctor or professor even in a just society. Did the intellectuals see factory workers from the perspective of equality in the former USSR? My answer is 'no'. Theory is all about knowing things but understanding is all about realisation. Realising the fact that all of us are fundamentally equal is spirituality. I often see intellectuals enjoying their intellectual status but disguising it with pseudo modesty, and at the same time talking about equality. These things happened even in the USSR. No communist movement in the world so far has witnessed equal respect for mental labour and physical labour. All communist parties in India have their 'intellectual cell'. Other political parties have their 'think tank'. It is as if a labourer cannot think, and as if by being blind followers for ages the people in the margins have forgotten how to articulate the thoughts they have at any time in any space. In India Marxism is an elite subject. The Communist Party never tried to take Marx's idea to the common people. As a result we see workers who inside the factory are members of left trade unions, but outside they vote for Shiv Sena [Ed: hard-line fundamentalist Hindu party]; they are divided along caste lines, party lines, religious lines, racial lines. You find unity inside factories or at the workplace and alienation outside in the society. (Understanding of oneness among workers did not develop even in the USSR. I certainly don't expect to find oneness between capitalists and their workers.) Even the thinkers from the subaltern section we knew are mostly forgotten nowadays. So economic equality is not total equality. To establish total equality we have to change our perspective about people. In the so-called socialist world there was some measure of economic equality, but there were a lot of other inequalities. I feel that scientific socialism is based fundamentally on the principle of 'each according to your need'. The income question does not arise there, the only question is need. In Islam we find the same concept of each according to your need. There are a lot of socialist elements in the philosophy of Islam. True Islamic practice is quite compatible with socialist thought like the thought of Vedanta, which says everyone is the son of Amrita, which says '*tatmawasi*'[1]: you are God. To establish the principle of each according to your need one needs to overcome the influence of self-interest. Overcoming self-interest is not a theoretical move, it is a spiritual journey based on the realisation that we are one. Spirituality is inbuilt in the concept of scientific socialism. Vivekananda had a pragmatic view also. He did not interpret only, changing the society mattered to him. He said: 'go to the people, give them information, develop their intellectual faculty'; he himself went to the downtrodden people. Throughout his short life he got himself involved deeply with activism.

Clément: The point is you make a connection between the spirituality of Vivekananda and the method of Boal?

Sanjoy: Yes, Boal says essentially what Paulo Freire said: people have enormous possibility. Human beings are capable of thinking and making mistakes. In many ways they have said the same thing: what they wanted was to create a space for dialogue. And Vivekananda said the same thing. He was against dictating, he believed that people can learn by themselves, what they need is information which they are deprived of. In a class-divided society information is capitalised within a class. Some people have more information, more knowledge, some people have little. That is the character of the class-divided society. In order to establish equality, first recognise the intellectual ability of the people. If there is an intellectual equality, then true equality is just a matter of time.

Clément: Can you develop a little bit more about this question of space? Because last time we spoke about this intellectual ability of the people and you came to a point where you said that to turn this theory into practice we need to create a space.

Sanjoy: Yes: a saint in Varanasi told my friend from America that thought evolves when people mingle. Where do people mingle? In a space created from the urge to mingle. When we want to discuss, the very desire for discussion creates a space. We create space through our theatre. Vivekananda appealed to the youth to go to the villages with a globe, some chemicals, a camera. I don't know why he suggested a camera. Probably he wanted to make use of the medium to provide an opportunity for the reflection which people require in their life. He is the one who said that India will emerge from the huts of the underprivileged. Here is what he said, clearly addressing the upper-class elite: 'Let New India arise – out of the peasants' cottage, grasping the plough; out of the huts of the fisherman, the cobbler, and the sweeper. Let her spring from the grocer's shop, from beside the oven of the fritter-seller. Let her emanate from the factory, from marts, and from markets. Let her emerge from groves and forests, from hills and mountains . . . '

Clément: You are saying class but what about the caste system?

Sanjoy: Indian society is divided into caste and in his time the caste system was even stronger. Here most people belong to the lower caste and at the same time to the lower economic class. In his time the two things were seen as one. He thus made no difference between caste and class. His theory of a *sudra* [Ed: servant caste] uprising was basically a class struggle in the Indian context. And he was against the caste system. There are many examples of this. So he says that *brahmins* [Ed: priestly/intellectual caste] will disappear. He told that caste to get ready, that the *sudra*, the subaltern people will expose you. And if you don't want to be exposed by them, recognise this subaltern community. In the parliament of religions in Chicago in 1893, he said: 'the crying evil in the East is not religion – they have religion enough – but it is bread that the suffering millions of burning India cry out for with parched throats. They ask us for bread, but we give them stones. It is an insult to a starving people to offer them religion; it is an insult to a starving man to teach him metaphysics'. So he was not ritualistic, he didn't speak like a leader of an organised religion. In many ways he was more revolutionary than the revolutionaries in India at his time.

He also said: 'I have seen your Parliament, Senate, Vote, Ballot, Majority. The same situation is true everywhere in the world, a few powerful men are running the society, all the others are a flock of sheep.' He believed that unless there is spiritual awakening, political freedom will be for a few elites. I take this statement seriously after the fall of the Socialist bloc. I have explained that his spirituality was in no way connected with organised religion. As he said in his speech in Chicago: 'Sectarianism, bigotry, and its horrible descendant, fanaticism, have long possessed this beautiful earth. They have filled the earth with violence, drenched it often and often with human blood, destroyed civilisation and sent whole nations to despair. Had it not been for these horrible demons, human society would be far more advanced than it is now'. Do you see that modern civilisation is progressing in that sense? He always explained how physics and metaphysics complement each other in the journey of understanding the Truth. He criticised the Church vehemently for acting against scientific discoveries and progress. He was the most eminent personality of his time who felt the need for scientific research.

Clément: I have too many questions to ask. Yesterday we spoke about the difference between *Shonar Meye* and *Monsanto*. In the play *Monsanto*, you give information, but in *Shonar Meye*, you don't give information. You just show a part of village life.

Sanjoy: There is nothing wrong in giving information, the problem lies in showing '*the* way'. In *Shonar Meye* we proposed to people to think about three phases of women's life by portraying different scenes in an episodic manner. We learnt this episodic form from the *Gajan*, a traditional theatre form in rural Bengal.

But in the play on the new green revolution where you found a discussion of Monsanto's role, this was different because we were dealing with some scientific technological subject where we had to give some concrete information. What Monsanto is, what GM food is, what scientists are saying etc. is not known to our audience yet. So to take the dialogue forward we had to do it. But the questions in the Monsanto play we opened to the spect-actors were concrete and clear. We asked our audience: 'do you think this is how you can develop your agriculture and do you think this development can give you a human culture, can make you independent?' In both plays there was a portrayal of facts of life that affect us and may make us oppressed. The spectators were informed and not unduly influenced one way or the other.

Clément: Last time when you spoke about Vivekananda, after five minutes of discussion you spoke about the book *The Imitation of Christ*. Can you develop why, in this discussion, you cited this reference?

Sanjoy: To me *The Imitation of Christ* is a fascinating text. I think Vivekananda made me interested in Christ, Mohammed and Buddha. Because he actually spoke highly about them. I see Christ as the first political activist, who adopted the tactic of non-violence and got assassinated by the state. The journey of socialism started with Buddha in Asia.

Clément: Perhaps it's a good thing to imitate Vivekananda?

Sanjoy: No, that question does not arise. You may not like all he said or practised. You don't have to – blind following and blind rejection are both unscientific. You cannot understand him unless you argue for and against him. To understand Vivekananda you have to consider him like your friend and you have to argue against him. He was very argumentative, he used to challenge others, to debate with Sri Ramakrishna, who considered the *guru* system a form of prostitution. He did not want to be a *guru*. His association with Sri Ramakrishna made the English-educated rationalist Vivekananda understand democracy.

He never publicised Sri Ramakrishna. And many people in India criticised him because he never talked about Ramakrishna in Europe. And in answer he said: 'they have Christ, why should I talk about Ramakrishna there?' It is not the person but the idea which is important. Girish Chandra, playwright, director, actor and composer, who became a legend in the nineteenth century, should be mentioned here. Girish Chandra was once talking to his actors. He was saying to them to just remember Ramakrishna and nothing else to enjoy peace in life. Girish used to respect Ramakrishna blindly, he had complete submission. Vivekananda was present and he called out to Girish Chandra personally and said: 'don't say this. I love purity'. It is not Ramakrishna but his ideas which are important. So he was against personification. You have to understand this. Marxists here have made Marx and Engels their God. But they often talk against religious fundamentalism. I often say in my workshops: 'I am giving you a fish, leave the bones and take the flesh.' People appreciate it very much. But it was actually said by Sri Ramakrishna. I don't quote or mention him when I say this, particularly in the West. I want to avoid misunderstanding, I am not his propagandist. Sri Ramakrishna and Vivekananda do not need propaganda any more than the sun. The sun gives us light and life. Does the sun need any propaganda? Every particle in this earth knows and feels the sun.

Clément: In your book [Ed: Routledge 2010], you say that spirituality 'is direct experience of human potential in relation to others and to the world'. How would you define this relation?

Sanjoy: I think collectivism comes from the feeling of oneness. Without the feeling of oneness we can act jointly and this can be called joint social action. In joint social action individuals act with common self-interest – for example, a strike for better wages, which everyone joins for their individual interest; some call it collective self-interest. In this instance we do not transcend caste, religion and other divisive factors. Workers fight against the owner inside the factory but outside they practise the caste system or follow fundamentalists. To go from joint social action to collective action is the journey of feeling oneness: and that's spirituality to me, where we construct true relationship, we create connection. Theatre of the Oppressed is the politics of creating connection. It takes us from collective self-interest to collectivism.

Clément: But the relation between humans is not always a good relation, an agreeable relation. In the last forum of *Shonar Meye*, the man who came on stage said things you did not agree with. So your understanding of relation also needs to be able to accept this person.

Sanjoy: When I say connection it doesn't mean that you will have no difference with others' perspective or position. The friction between two stones makes fire; in difference, in friction, in conflict, thought evolves. So we invite conflicts in order to understand the truth, not to win the argument. Attempting to win an argument isolates us, whereas argument to develop critical understanding integrates thoughts and connects us. The objective of establishing a position by hook or by crook makes us dogmatic: then dialogues among us become multiple monologues. Dialogue demands connection, Theatre of the Oppressed demands connection among people experiencing different forms of oppression at the margins of society.

Clément: What does Vivekananda say about argument?

Sanjoy: Vivekananda was against all sorts of fundamentalism, religious fundamentalism in particular. In his Chicago speech in 1893 he said: 'Superstition is bad but religious fundamentalism is even worse'. He was very argumentative, a great debater and encouraged debate and argument throughout his life. The modern development paradigm wants to uniformise the world. The didactic concept of one development, one culture is imposed on every nation by the modern pattern of globalisation. There is no recognition of diversity. The fact is unity cannot exist without the existence of diversified culture, a diversified concept of development, a diversified attitude towards life. This modern aggressive capitalism gives no importance to this diversity and that's how this system is digging its own grave.

Clément: My last question is a metaphysical question, an abstract question. What is the limit of this spirituality? What is the limit of this kind of relationship?

Sanjoy: Spirituality is a journey from limited to unlimited, from 'I' to 'we', from being to becoming, as Vivekananda said. Aggressive capitalism will never encourage this spirituality, as it goes against individualism. Capital wants alienation, individualism for its market to exist; all organised religions survive with the support of this system because they divide people.

Clément: After twenty-nine years' experience, are you able to learn from people who have just five years of experience?

Sanjoy: I often learn from the people, young and elderly. I love questions more than the answers. Because the questions make me think, help me to develop an understanding about the issues we want to address. I feel blessed as I can learn from people, young, old, privileged and marginal.

This is true of society also. Even after a socialist revolution, society will not be static, society has to move further. We must remember revolution is also a journey of dynamic evolution. Even in theatre we cannot create a static image. Any apparently static image is a result of dynamic thought, thought is evolution and therefore we can bring change by using a static image, producing a new one and then changing it again. Theatre for change or for revolution will never end its journey. We cannot deny the theory of evolution which was not only biological but also psychological.

Note

1 This phrase often appears as *tatwa twam asi* (Ed.).

The political aesthetic of Jana Sanskriti
Theatre as an art of creating connection

Sanjoy Ganguly

> In this essay: (a) readers will find the scope of theatre I have perceived; (b) they will see how spect-activists are created; (c) they will see the integration of the words collective, connection and oneness with the concept of Jana Sanskriti's theatre. The essay also sums up many of the positions expressed in the preceding interviews.

In an essay in *Scripting Power: Jana Sanskriti On and Offstage* (2010), Ralph Yarrow asks 'What next?' for Jana Sanskriti, the movement I have directed since 1985. According to him, Jana Sanskriti exemplifies:

A practice of theatre
A social and communal ethics
A political strategy
An educational model
A local, regional, national and international symbolic function (Yarrow in Da Costa 2010, 191)

How do these features of Jana Sanskriti's work exemplify a political aesthetic and how does this support its vision for the near future?

In the same book, Dia Da Costa says that Jana Sanskriti practises theatre which 'squarely refuse[s] the foreclosure of our imaginations' (Da Costa 2010, 9) and indicates that the actors' stories reproduced there 'speak of the concomitant push of poverty and the pull and promise of learning, opportunities, fun, feeling valued and gaining self-confidence' (12); for her, Jana Sanskriti's work creates 'spect-actor[s] of history . . . who engage in constant critical play on and offstage by upsetting the assumed boundaries between fiction and reality, in order to construct social change [and] to rejuvenate political struggle itself' (16).

One of the major ways in which Jana Sanskriti achieves this is by creating an aesthetic of relationship (in training and rehearsal and in performance). Here, aesthetics means extension of sense, of possibilities of meaning, of different approaches to issues and situations materialised in practice. The results of this development (a form of Freirian literacy, a pedagogy of the oppressed which has respect for intellect and rationality at its core) can be seen in spect-actors' communities and are embedded in management structures. It is a form of democracy in action.

'Thought evolves when people mingle', said a stranger in Varanasi to my friend. When I heard this, I felt that this is what inspires us to make theatre. In theatre people mingle, actors propose, provoke the audience to think. Actors and spectators think together, the journey for the spectators and actors to the world of thought starts and continues in theatre.

'Why do we Europeans always suffer from fear?', a young man asked me at a conference in Vienna. I was initially unable to answer his question, thought a while, and remembered the stranger in Varanasi. 'Yes, it is the fence of individualism around us. We have put ourselves into the prison of individualism, alienation breeds fear and pessimism, hope exists in connection', I replied. Isn't theatre hope?

But what is connection? How does it get constructed? Are there any preconditions? I would like to tell the story of Mullah Nasiruddin here. It's a story I read. Some people think Nasiruddin was a sufi who lived in Turkey. One day he set off from his village to a distant place where his teacher Murshid used to live. Nasiruddin walked for three days to reach the doorstep of his teacher's house. After arriving, he knocked at the door.

From inside the house Murshid replied: 'Is there anybody there outside?'

Nasiruddin replied: 'Yes sir, I am Nasiruddin waiting at your doorstep.'

This question and answer between teacher and disciple was repeated several times. But the door did not open for Nasiruddin. Nasiruddin got very upset about it, he came from a very distant village, he was in pain. He started thinking too and after some time he decided to go and knock again at the door of his teacher Murshid.

Murshid replied from inside the house: 'Is there anybody there outside?'

Nasiruddin answered: 'It is you waiting outside.'

This time the door opened.

We can see the message clearly. In a relationship, there should be no separation between 'I' and 'You'. The construction of a relationship is a journey from 'I' to 'You'. In Theatre of the Oppressed, we need to combat the hierarchy between actors and spectators. It is essentially a journey from 'I' to you, an art of creating connection, a construction of relationship between actors and spectators. We learn in this relationship. Theatre of the Oppressed is an art of learning.

What do we mean by learning? Can we propose something to our spectators which they don't know? Impossible! In TO, those who are oppressed act as actors and spectators. The oppression portrayed in the scene is an oppression which actors and spectators live, they experience it all the time, at every moment. What we show in the play is known to actors and spectators. Here the actors and spectators understand what they already know. Knowing and understanding are similar but they are very different too. For example, a scene of domestic violence shows nothing new to the people, we all know this. But in a Forum theatre session, actors and spectators understand how patriarchy operates in the psyche of an oppressive husband and how patriarchy is even internalised within women as a value of life.

In Forum theatre, actors and spectators witness a debate between oppressor characters and 'spect-actors' who replace the oppressed. Each time a new spect-actor comes on stage, the debate either raises new questions or adds new dimensions to the whole argument of oppression shown in the play. The joker throws those questions to the house. Spect-actors take up those questions and use them to structure their interventions, and as a result the debate keeps getting extended. In the process, the house experiences oppressor characters who justify their actions by recourse to different kinds of logic; this reflects how patriarchy acts as an internalised doctrine in the psyche of the oppressors in the society. Similarly, by seeing spect-actors intervening as the protagonist, a real oppressed woman in the audience who thinks that her duty is to serve her husband unconditionally, who has up to now accepted that she can be mentally tortured or even beaten up by her husband, understands how she carries in herself the baggage of patriarchal norms and ideology. The traditional upbringing of girl children often turns a woman into a follower of patriarchal values. When an oppressed woman recognises herself in the actions of spect-actors who are trying to change the situation, the truth suddenly becomes clear to her. She becomes the spectator of her own actor in real life. This introspection creates a desire for deconstruction of the values that were constructed in her, perhaps from her childhood.

It is important both in Forum theatre and in other forms of TO to understand that TO is not a problem-solving session, we cannot solve all the problems of our lives on stage. Seeing TO as a problem-solving session narrows down the whole politics of TO. It is about understanding what we know. It is an intellectual journey where actors and 'spect-actors' join and develop a deeper understanding of the oppression. This gives a critical view of the power relations we experience inside the family and outside in the broader world. We portray domestic violence in order to understand how patriarchy operates within us as a doctrine. This is what can be called a journey from effect to cause, from result to reason, from experience to theory, from concrete to abstract. In this intellectual journey, actors and spectators evolve, they experience intellectual development taking place within them.

But also, the actors and spectators can feel this development within them. Aesthetics does not come from seeing only, it is also an act of feeling. This is the aesthetics of Theatre of the Oppressed to me: here everyone on stage and in the audience feels the evolution of their intellect. Aesthetics is an art of learning.

In this way, TO and Forum theatre in particular script intellectual power on stage. We all know that the stage gets extended to the whole space in the theatre while we 'Forum' with the 'spect-actors'. The intellectual power we script on stage breaks the passivity, makes actors and spectators active off the stage, transforming spect-actors into *spect-activists*, actors into activists.

Let me cite an example. In India there is a public food distribution system where we find a lot of corruption involved. There are shops in the cities and villages called ration shops run by dealers appointed by the government. Ration cards are issued by the food and supply department of the respective areas. Every citizen is entitled to have a card, child and adults, young and elderly, men and women, everyone. Mostly the underprivileged population goes to the ration shop in their area. In a ration shop, cardholders get food grains at a subsidised price. There are some special benefits given to citizens living below the poverty line. Jana Sanskriti once made a play on how dealers cheat deprived beneficiaries who are poor, underprivileged and often illiterate. We presented a concrete situation of oppression. We performed the play in twenty-five villages; in each case we performed the same play to the same group of spectators three times with an interval of a month between the shows. While conducting Forum sessions, we noticed spectators often pointing out the basic lacunas in the food policy of the government. Our play acted as an intellectual space where spectators and actors debated about a concrete oppression and identified the root cause. After about one hundred performances we organised a couple of seminars on the food policy of our country, in which noted economists confirmed the problems expressed in the interventions made by our spectators during one hundred Forum theatre sessions. (Each satellite team of Jana Sanskriti in the villages has a writer who documents the interventions of the spect-actors with their names and addresses. This written documentation of interventions is carefully kept in the library of Jana Sanskriti for researchers.)

The spect-actors act off the stage after an intensive brain-storming in the Forum theatre session. In this case they organised a deputation to the officials of the department of food and supply and convinced local government to arrange a meeting between ration dealers and villagers; under the pressure of our spect-activists and activists a monitoring committee was set up, comprising villagers and government officials.

Political aesthetic of Jana Sanskriti 137

This intellectual journey also gives an experience of aesthetics. Aesthetics is not just about seeing, it is also about feeling, understanding; aesthetics is an art of understanding what we already know, what was already there unknown to us. The law of gravity was already there, it was not waiting to be discovered by Newton, as Vivekananda said. For Newton, the fall of an apple was a proposition, of the same kind as those made by Forum theatre. Newton used the knowledge he already had to understand the new phenomenon. That is what happens in Forum theatre. Actors propose what people experience daily, then actors and spect-actors try to understand the phenomena they see and hear. The understanding they arrive at together is a collective learning, a collective action. That is the greatest dimension of aesthetics I see in TO.

In an interview my friend Robert asked: 'Boal called the Theatre of the Oppressed a "rehearsal for revolution"; nowadays we often say a "rehearsal for reality". In Jana Sanskriti you say it's a "rehearsal for the total revolution". What does that mean?' I said in reply: 'With total revolution we mean people evolving as intellectuals. When actors and spectators develop a sociological understanding of their issues, they experience intellectual growth. That is what we call internal revolution. That breaks the passivity. That inspires them to go for an external revolution. So we are saying it's a total revolution.'

The internal revolution is important for the external revolution. If the external revolution happens without the internal revolution, you are speaking *for* the people instead of letting them speak for themselves. Internal revolution ensures the manifestation of the intellectual faculty every one of us has within. Forum theatre in particular creates an intellectual discourse where actors and spectators are provoked to think critically about the oppression portrayed in the play. Each intervention comes from rational thinking, as opposed to blind following of social and political institutions and conventions. Therefore, when people act off the stage to change their reality after experiencing a debate and critical dialogue on stage, that becomes a Politics of the Oppressed. Here actors off the stage participate, based on their intellectual critical position on the issue. (This aspect of participation based on critical thinking is usually absent from conventional political practices. Instead, we often hear voices claiming to speak for the people, but in this situation, the oppressed are relegated to the position of mere followers and robbed of any agency of their own.) It is important that everyone experiences this internal revolution.

The Theatre of the Oppressed movement should take care of both aspects, internal and external revolution, which make up the total revolution, aesthetics as well as politics.

We have theorised that theatre is a collective action. The biggest challenge is therefore to realise what this implies in practice, in particular in terms of our understanding of the role of the joker. Often in Forum theatre the joker is given the most importance. No one can deny the role of the joker in TO. But for spectators, this is not a big question. More and more I feel it is a burning question for people within the TO community. For the spectators, the oppression shown in the play is most important. It is the actors who show the oppression on stage and engage spectators with the oppressive situation which needs to be discussed and debated through the dialogue in the Forum. Then the antagonist character takes the responsibility of problematising the interaction between spect-actors and the oppressor character. All these things enable the joker to go ahead and facilitate the Forum session. An excellent joker concentrates on discovering good questions which emerge during the multiple interaction between spect-actors and characters on stage. He or she throws these questions to the spectators, some spectators feel like addressing them and the transformation from spectators to spect-actors takes place, spect-actors come into being. So my point here is to see theatre, and Forum theatre in particular, as a collective action where everyone is equally important. By making the joker more important, we often inculcate patriarchy in our practice. Patriarchy is all about inequality. If we lack understanding about how patriarchy operates within us in a multidimensional way, we lose connection.

When I say theatre is an art of creating connection that means also the construction of a collective, both within the group of artists and between the artists and the spectators. Jana Sanskriti's practice of decision making and the allocation of roles and responsibilities within the core group, as well as its development of village- and area-level spect-actors' committees, provides a structure for this which has evolved over nearly thirty years of practice. It occurs also in daily performance experience.

Sometimes we perform in a village square, in a small circle with no sound system. The spectators donate hours of their time to this interactive dialogic space, even after the inhuman struggle of existence which they have to confront as part of their everyday lives. At a performance – certainly the first of its kind – in a very small village in the poorly resourced *adivasi* district of Purulia in early 2015, spectators immediately recognised that here was a format which, unlike any political or communal event they had previously experienced, offered them a chance to express their own views and become participants in a debate about issues which affected their lives. They were expressing their need for democracy, and in that moment for them, dialogue was a need felt by their heart. Of course the head has a role, but head and heart are there in connection, just as they are connected physiologically.

It is also quite common to give theoretical recognition to the intellectual faculty of 'the people'. But we fail to acknowledge its true value because we do not ask why people possess the desire for a dialogic space. Why has democracy always been the need of the people? The very desire signifies the intellectual faculty of the people, which often may remain undiscovered by people living at the margins for lack of opportunity. It is the recognition of this desire which needs to take precedence for TO practitioners. This is far more important than counting the number of interventions from the spect-actors or trying to make theatre a problem-solving session. These mistakes arise from our lack of understanding about what collective action is.

The contribution of 'the people' to Boal's structuring of Forum theatre is undeniable. Boal is a Freirian: for him theory originates from practice. The contribution of the spectators in making Boal think this way signifies his understanding of the intellectual need of the people. A good joker knows the art of listening. He or she should have the ability to empty herself/himself while listening to the debate between spect-actors and actors. After listening to them, the joker has to analyse the essence of the debate simply in order to discover good questions, certainly not in order to make statements or declare his/her own position. True listening is the pre-condition for dialogue. Otherwise it will become multiple monologue. As practitioners of TO we need to liberate ourselves from this culture of making multiple monologues which appear superficially to be dialogue. The big challenge is to evolve as a community; and that means remaining aware of this requirement at all levels of our operation. Let us be optimistic.

Art is social metaphor, theatre is political social thought reflected in the form of plays. When we use our play as means to dialogue with our spectators, it becomes a way to include everyone in the world of intellect. This is not just a comfort zone for the privileged, it is the right and the capacity of all human beings. Modern development paradigms and so-called democratic centralism tend not to recognise this truth.

Establishing equality does not mean fighting economic disparity *only*, it is about respecting differences of perception of life. It is an art of acceptance, it is an art of liberation from ego, from the 'I'; and above all it is fighting disparity in the world of intellect and establishing intellectual equality. Democracy as opposed to domination and imposition cannot be established unless we achieve this. The intellectual progress of individuals is the key to liberation. The process and action of liberation starts from intellectual movement. Here lies the relevance of TO.

Jana Sanskriti's everyday practice has been and is rooted in these lessons. Now Jana Sanskriti is building on this by establishing an International Resource and Research Centre. This will be both a physical and an intellectual space for dialogue and exchange. It aims to support exploration of all the above dimensions of connection through theory and practice. It will welcome investigation into all aspects of the practice of TO and related forms of applied and socially relevant theatre and will particularly seek to stimulate 'south-south' encounters. Thus it will be open to practitioners and researchers from the global spectrum of theatre and performance work which engages with social change, immediate issues and their structural causes. It will encourage practitioners and scholars to recognise each others' perspectives and approaches, to share them and to shape them in new ways.

This Centre, which will be launched in 2015, arises from the perceptions set out in my essay and aims to embody those principles. Maybe it can be seen as a space for play, in the most profound sense of the word recognised by Indian aesthetics. *Lila* means both 'a play' and 'the play of forces'; it is openness to each other and to new ways of combining thought and practice. Jana Sanskriti's aesthetic of connection and relationship is both a political and an artistic action which the founding of the Centre is intended to further materialise and sustain.

Coda
'Aesthetics as transformation'

Sanjoy Ganguly

In my understanding, aesthetics is a kind of knowing. Art is a key modality in the transformation of information into knowledge and the transformation of the subjects who experience this; I believe it is integral to the process of human development and signals a universal human capacity to engage intellectually and practically in the construction of human society. Acquiring information through engagement with art is also a dialectical process (a combination of observing and questioning) which shifts thinking to another stage.

In my first book I say:

> Actually collective initiative and action, debate, discussion, and intellectual exercise have been humanity's treasures since the early stages of human civilisation. In modern times only a few have access to the arena of cultural and intellectual activities. How will such a society preserve a human face?
>
> (Ganguly 2010, 144)

Sir Julian Huxley said: 'Man's evolution is not biological but psycho-social; it operates by the mechanism of cultural tradition, which involves the cumulative self-reproduction and self-variation of mental activities and their products. Accordingly, major steps in the human phase of evolution are achieved by breakthroughs to new dominant patterns of mental organization of knowledge, ideas and beliefs – ideological instead of physiological or biological organization' (Huxley 1960, 251–2). So he points out that knowledge evolves as a dialogic movement between what is already known and what is added to it. He further suggests that the ultimate aim of evolution is 'realisation of more possibilities', which is essentially an aesthetic process and emerges in all aesthetic production.

Aesthetics is a dialectical process of knowing – it is experience + new data > synthesis, i.e., it is organic (structural) and it produces a feeling of increased wholeness and coherence. Thus subsequently this feeling drives the desire (will) to make relationships between things, people and situations, so that feeling here is framed and focused by choice, the affective by the cognitive. The aesthetic as a mode of knowing is thus both sensitive and volitional. We experience, we recognise, we desire, we act, we create and we cohere.

In many cases TO – especially at early stages of practice – has tended to present simplistic and binary oppositions in a 'documentary' style which limits the possibility of real debate but also closes down the possibilities of experiencing and evaluating the situation through different kinds of information (channels of transmission) and thus awakening different kinds of knowing. This in effect means that the potentialities of theatre/drama as a form of communication are reduced, and instead of Theatre of the Oppressed there is something more like sloganeering of the Oppressed.

In saying 'We have within us such a wealth of possibilities!' (1995, 36), Boal recognises the fact that the creative nature of human beings is not a product of social forces, it is endemic. Social forces have tended to restrict and channel the scope of creativity to specific ends and ultimately to impose an economic paradigm which preaches didactic politics and robotises human beings. But on the other hand there are forces present in human nature which can decondition mind and thought, and theatre acts as an agent that switches on this process of reconditioning. The aesthetic is thus not just a feeling, not only the light that expresses the inner truth of a matter as Socrates said, it is a feeling connected to broader concrete political action; not just form, but the sum of form and content, will and objective, feeling and concrete action. Art evolved as a language of ideas, an evolution both biological and psychological in nature.

Aesthetic acts are also volitional: they involve choice and direction. They are therefore inherently political. It is therefore important to preserve the possibility of choosing action and direction, and in order for this to be meaningful there must be a viable spectrum of choice. Therefore two criteria are important for TO: (i) a range of aesthetic channels – style of performance, symbolic moments, attention to all performance elements, semiotic richness; and (ii) a spectrum of possibilities for interrogating the situation via Forum interventions and then subsequently for exploring how to address it in the daily life of the spect-actor community.

Aesthetics are thus vital to our operation. Two of the distinguishing features of our plays are folk elements and Forum, both of which function to promote engagement and judgement. Jana Sanskriti developed a structure for their plays which was not found in the Indian street theatre movement before. [Ed: see discussion in Ganguly 2010 for more on the development of 'street theatre' and its relationship to IPTA, the Indian People's Theatre Association

Coda: aesthetics as transformation 143

linked to the Communist Party of India] Street theatre mostly used propaganda plays in which the message was all important. It had structural rather than aesthetic beauty. Aesthetic beauty consists of more than structure, it is multi-dimensional and more nuanced, inviting a more complex response from spectators.

Folk theatre was a strong influence on Jana Sanskriti's theatre. Some of the actors had skills (song, dance, comic routines) found in it; and it was through observing folk artists that I as director began my own journey, having had no prior training in theatre. Secondly, folk theatre is very episodic in nature; a number of different stories are connected in one single piece. The characters in folk theatre are not perfect, they display both vices and virtues, very Brechtian in nature. 'Jana Sanskriti views classical and folk theatre as valuable because they represent complex characters – whether Gods, humans, nature, and kings – each with myriad faults, fallibility, powers and agency. This complexity of the characters incites critical thinking among the audience because it disables outright empathy for any one character, heroic or otherwise' (Ganguly 2009, 10). Here beauty is structural as well as intellectual. In avoiding empathising, so-called 'illiterate' people here become critics of the characters usually shown in folk theatre. This criticality is the positive conflict between internal and external reality and represents a further dimension of the aesthetics of thinking which is developed in our workshops and performances.

A scene from *Village Dream*

Postscript
A critical space
Forum, jokering and the problem of sympathy

Sanjoy Ganguly

> We are all, in different ways, trapped into kinds of thinking and behaving, into positions and roles and attitudes. Whatever the cause – internalisation of behaviour patterns or values, oppression by circumstances or systems – it is important to make use of the methods of Forum to begin to break free from these patterns rather than to reinforce them. This requires a high degree of vigilance from performers, jokers and specta(c)tors. (Ed.)

Before this manuscript was completed, the launch of the Jana Sanskriti International Research and Resource Institute (JSIRRI) occurred in December 2015. Its vision and mission statement was drafted by delegates present at the first international meeting at Jana Sanskriti's base in Badu. One key clause articulates the need for theatre to interact with other disciplines in the social sciences. Another highlights the importance of negotiating with other forms of political theatre and models of applied theatre and to include them in the remit of JSIRRI. I value this latter aim very highly.

It is a recognition of the degree to which we have all become victims of political and social structures which alienate us from each other. Even as practitioners of methods which aim to assist people to identify and address issues and problems in their lives and to find ways of moving beyond them, it is often difficult to avoid functioning as part of the competitive machine which pits one 'producer' against another; and which has often turned creative arts into commodities for sale rather than means to emancipation and connection. So this statement signals a realisation that, as a community of practitioners, we need to reclaim the ethics and strategies of interconnection and democratic dialogue. We need to use our own work and the work of others as ways of becoming spectators of our own actions in this field too.

I recently attended a Forum theatre festival in Europe. One of the plays was about an immigrant from Africa, who had come to Europe but found that his qualifications were not recognised and he could not get a job. The content and structure of the piece were fine. The protagonist came across as someone who felt excluded and lost.

The joker came on stage and asked for interventions from the spectators. One spectator came and offered the protagonist a cup of coffee. The protagonist replied: 'what will happen to me after we have drunk the coffee?' The interventionist spectator had no answer. A second spectator came up; he also did not replace the protagonist. He took the role of a busy man on the street, a privileged white man. He offered the protagonist lodging at his home for a couple of days. The protagonist replied: 'but I need a place to stay. What if I can't stay at your home until I get a job?' The interventionist spectator looked visibly helpless. Up to this point spectators were attempting to genuinely feel the situation of the protagonist. But the joker did not attempt to transform the Forum theatre session into a political enquiry. It could have been a space to understand the role of modern capital, the concept of the nation state, the economy of war, etc. But neither the actors nor the joker were equipped to do this. This is where I think play-making needs to include a rigorous process to understand the situation of oppression portrayed in the play from all possible social, economic and political dimensions. And Forum theatre is not necessarily a problem-solving session; rather it is important to understand it as a way of developing a critical political understanding of the oppressive situation in question.

Another spectator came on stage and asked the protagonist, quite aggressively: 'don't you know your diploma is valid here too?' The main oppressed character replied that he had been several times to the job centre, and each time his application had been rejected. The spect-actor refused to believe the oppressed character in the play. After this there was an overflowing of sympathy from the spectators to the main oppressed character. But the joker did not know how to tackle the situation and the Forum ended.

I want to make one thing very clear. Sympathy is a form of patronisation so long as we are unable to truly feel the situation of the people living in oppression. A momentary feeling of sympathy makes virtually no sense; rather, it is an insult to the oppressed. It does not inspire us to take appropriate action. True sympathy comes from a feeling of oneness and that requires us to move beyond our class or role or status, to engage in whatever way is possible with the lived reality of those who are exploited, who are oppressed, who live at the margins. The kind of sympathy shown in the Forum performance was at least a serious dilution of this oneness if not diametrically opposed to it.

On the next day of the festival a Palestinian-Israeli mixed group presented the problem of occupation. Four actors performed on two zones of the stage. In one zone a young Israeli boy tried to convince his father of the need to stop the occupation and create unity. On the other side a similar attempt was seen from a young Palestinian boy trying to convince his mother to go and negotiate with the Israelis and make friendship with them. The mother was connected to a Palestinian 'Jihadi' outfit. After the performance the joker asked the spectators to intervene. There were some Muslim youths in the audience: my guess is that their forefathers came to Europe probably many years before. Two of them intervened; they replaced the character of the Palestinian boy and tried to explain the need for peace and friendship with Israelis. They explained that they understood the need for peace and friendship through living in Europe for generations and that there is no need to lose friends and relatives in the war. Then a few interventions came from the European audience; these simply taught the Palestinian mother like teachers in a school that she should not have become involved in Jihad, as if the thinking which had brought her to this was very simply constructed with no rhyme or reason and could be deconstructed magically. In this way, some spectators unknowingly closed off all opportunities to talk about the sociology and politics of the genesis of the problem, by adopting this teaching mode. And the joker did not pick this up. We should essentially focus on opening more doors and windows for actors and spectators to create more opportunities for intellectual discourse in the Forum theatre session, rather than making it a place for showcasing our virtues and/or our superior 'knowledge'.

After the show was over I was standing outside the auditorium and a friend from Bolivia came up to me. He was visibly disturbed and said: 'Sanjoy, what we saw today in the theatre was a colonial expression of solidarity, we need to decolonise the concept of solidarity.' I am strongly in agreement with what he said. We need to work to free Theatre of the Oppressed from this kind of pollution and make it a true political space for understanding our reality as the first step towards a change.

At this point, the point Joschka from Austria made should be mentioned. Joschka presented another complex dimension to this whole discourse. After seeing the play on the conflict between Palestinians and Israelis, Joschka said: 'As a German I have always had a sympathy for Jews that sometimes functions as a hurdle to understand the whole question of the occupation problem in Palestine/Israel. If an interactive play cannot help me to identify my construction of thought as a block to understanding the whole issue, then what is this theatre for?'

Both in our plays and in our workshops, we need to respect and to deploy the essential nature of Boal's theatre practice: to problematise, to ask questions about our situations, our assumptions, our practices and our world.

Letters from Augusto Boal and Sanjoy Ganguly, March/April 2009

[*Editor's Note:* These letters offer a snapshot of (i) the relationship between Boal and Ganguly and (ii) some of the pressures and issues involved in attempting to combine active fieldwork with the desire to create an international forum for discussion and development of TO practice in the world. This issue is also discussed on pages 146–8 of Ganguly's book (see below).]

On 2 March 2009 Sanjoy Ganguly wrote:

Respectable Boal,[1] Hope you are well. I am sorry that I could not pay much attention to the forthcoming meeting in Rio. I just did not find time to pause for a moment since last November. The work is expanding, a lot of problems of various kind as usual. Sometimes I get so tired that I feel like retiring now. I am going to be 50 soon but I sometimes feel as if I am above 71 years old. My capacity is limited but still I cannot take a break from my work in Theatre and politics.

I am now in Canada to talk about ToO and the practice done by Jana Sanskriti. It is also a fund raising for me.

In between I sent to you the edited version of my book. I did not get any reply from you. My last 23 years in theatre and politics and last 18 years in ToO likes to have a preface from you. I am sincerely expecting that you will include this in your urgent agenda, I am your best student urging to you.

All of us in Jana Sanskriti are well. With best regards.

Sanjoy.

On Friday, 6 March 2009 7:31 PM, Augusto Boal wrote:

Dear Sanjoy,

Right now, I am at the Hospital Samaritano. As you know, my disease is chronic and attacks me regularly – then, I have to slow down. I am writing you on my laptop but I cannot work long times. I promise you that I will write Talia Rodgers today to assure her that I am going to write a Preface to your book. This, I agree, can help her to make a favorable decision, but will not be decisive in publishing the book: Routledge will always think about the possibilities of selling – they are obviously in the market.

I will do my real best, believe me. I don't know yet how long I will stay here at this hospital.

All my very best wishes, fraternally,

Augusto

PS – don't complain about your age: you are very, very young and extraordinarily dynamic!!!! You will never retire!!!!!!!!!!!!!!!!

On Saturday, 7 March 2009 5:34 PM, Augusto Boal wrote:

Dear Sanjoy,

You are a wonderful person, an important man of the theatre, untiring worker, with an enormous capacity of organization. Theatre of the Oppressed needs you!!! Complain all that you want and need, and I will do all I can to help you, so much you have helped the development of Theatre of the Oppressed!

Fraternally to you and to your wonderful wife Shima, enormous artist and activist, from your elder brother, Augusto.

From Augusto Boal:

Dear Ronald, Adrian, Luc, Sanjoy, Julián,

Forgive my delay: I broke one small bone of my right hand which made me return to the emergency of Samaritano Hospital. Happily, I have a great majority of bones which are perfectly healthy; even in spite of my proud 78 years old, I have almost no osteoporosis at all!!!

This is a draft of a letter I intend to send around to all people who have shown interest in coming. Please return to me with your opinions before I leave to Paris next Friday. My idea would be to send one mail every three weeks to keep everyone informed.

Fraternally, Augusto

Rio de Janeiro, March 18th, 2009

Dear friends,

After exchanging opinions about our Project of Jokers in Rio July 2009, we decided that I should send to all of you, who have shown interest in participating, a personal mail, even though using such a collective non-personal way. I will tell you sincerely where things stand right now.

1. We are striving hard to find financial conditions to do that Meeting, which seems extremely important to all of us. Our main possible sponsors are the University of Rio and Serviço Social do Comércio (SESC). No one has as yet given their official support. Besides them, we are trying other organisations. Before the big neo-cannibal-liberal crisis, the possibilities of doing our Project looked very promising; now, not so brilliant, but still very possible. We are fighting for that, and FORMAAT is fighting for that too.
2. The main objectives of this Meeting will be to get together, to explain what we are doing with TO, what our problems have been, in which way our achievements can inspire all of us. This is a Meeting of Theatre of the Oppressed, which means to say that we are going to invite ONLY those people who practice Theatre of the Oppressed. I reinforce that because most of us know that there are some persons and some groups, in Europe, in the US and other places, who do whatever they want and call that TO, which is unfair and is not honest.
3. I ask personally to each one of you who will eventually come – even more, I ask my closest friends – to send us material about their work which, with your permission, will not be returned, but will be incorporated into the Boal Library at the University of Rio, open to the public. DVDs, videos, photos, newspapers, books, plays, films – everything that you find useful. This should be done imperatively BEFORE THE END OF APRIL, since it will be necessary and useful also to confirm the possible participation of those persons about whom we don't have enough information.
4. The participation will be in three levels:
    a) Those Jokers who we already know well, who frequently exchange information and experiences among ourselves. These will have time to expose their work to other participants in special moments, mainly in the mornings, answer questions, exchange. Eventually, these moments will or will not be opened to the general public;
    b) jokers who have not enough amount of information to share, but who will be admitted to all activities of the Meeting, specially in some presentations of our groups of TO;
    c) beginners who will be admitted as Observers.

Centro do Teatro do Oprimido (CTO), as of now, cannot assure anything more than our sincere good will. We don't have money to pay for travel, food,

lodging, nothing at all. But we keep trying, and will let you know of further developments on this side. According to the material we will receive from you before the end of April, we will organise a Program to discuss, in a parallel or continuous way – that depends on the material you will send us soon – themes like Violent Communities, Gender, Racism, Sexism, Economical Crisis and Neo-Liberalism, Land, Salaries and Workers, Rainbow of Desire, Legislative Theatre, Mental Health, Schools, Education and Pedagogy, etc.
Please, let me know your reactions.

friendly, Augusto Boal

The following text, Boal's speech to UNESCO on 27 March 2009, was sent to Ganguly at his request:

All human societies are "spectacular*" in their daily life and produce "spectacles" at special moments. They are "spectacular" as a form of social organization and produce "spectacles" like the one you have come to see.

Even if one is unaware of it, human relationships are structured in a theatrical way. The use of space, body language, choice of words and voice modulation, the confrontation of ideas and passions, everything that we demonstrate on the stage, we live in our lives. We are theatre!

Weddings and funerals are "spectacles", but so, also, are daily rituals so familiar that we are not conscious of this. Occasions of pomp and circumstance, but also the morning coffee, the exchanged good-mornings, timid love and storms of passion, a senate session or a diplomatic meeting – all is theatre.

One of the main functions of our art is to make people sensitive to the "spectacles" of daily life in which the actors are their own spectators, performances in which the stage and the stalls coincide. We are all artists. By doing theatre, we learn to see what is obvious but what we usually can't see because we are only used to looking at it. What is familiar to us becomes unseen: doing theatre throws light on the stage of daily life.

Last September, we were surprised by a theatrical revelation: we, who thought that we were living in a safe world, despite wars, genocide, slaughter and torture which certainly exist, but far from us in remote and wild places. We, who were living in security with our money invested in some respectable bank or in some honest trader's hands in the stock exchange were told that this money did not exist, that it was virtual, a fictitious invention by some economists who were not fictitious at all and neither reliable nor respectable. Everything was just bad theatre, a dark plot in which a few people won a lot and many people lost all.

Some politicians from rich countries held secret meetings in which they found some magic solutions. And we, the victims of their decisions, have remained spectators in the last row of the balcony.

Twenty years ago, I staged Racine's Phèdre in Rio de Janeiro. The stage setting was poor: cow skins on the ground, bamboos around. Before each presentation, I used to say to my actors: "The fiction we created day by day is over. When you cross those bamboos, none of you will have the right to lie. Theatre is the Hidden Truth".

When we look beyond appearances, we see oppressors and oppressed people, in all societies, ethnic groups, genders, social classes and castes; we see an unfair and cruel world. We have to create another world because we know it is possible. But it is up to us to build this other world with our hands and by acting on the stage and in our own life.

Participate in the "spectacle" which is about to begin and once you are back home, with your friends act your own plays and look at what you were never able to see: that which is obvious. Theatre is not just an event; it is a way of life!

We are all actors: being a citizen is not living in society, it is changing it.

Augusto Boal
(Original Portuguese)

* means also having the nature of a spectacle or show (translator's note)

And finally:

'I believe that what Richard Schechner said about Augusto Boal, my father, that 'he realized what Brecht just dreamt about' can be applied to Sanjoy Ganguly, he is the dream of my father. By the extent of his work, by the solidity of the mass movement he helped to create, by their eagerness in using theatre as a lever to change this world into a better one, Ganguly is, with or without a prize, a shining example that inspires all of us who believe a world of equals is possible.'

Julian Boal

Note

1 Sanjoy often writes this! The correct (though nowadays very rarely used) English would be 'Respected'. Indian English retains a number of stylistic formalities which are no longer in general use. (Ed.)

Bibliography

Boal, Augusto (1992) *Games for Actors and Non-Actors*, trans. Adrian Jackson. London: Routledge

Da Costa, Dia (2010) (Ed.) *Scripting Power: Jana Sanskriti On and Offstage*. Kolkata: Camp

Ganguly, Sanjoy (2009) *Where We Stand: Five Plays by Sanjoy Ganguly*. Kolkata: Camp

Ganguly, Sanjoy (2010) *Jana Sanskriti: Forum Theatre and Democracy in India*. London: Routledge

Vivekananda (1989) *Complete Works*, Vol. 1. Kolkata: Advaita Ashram

Yarrow, Ralph (2010) 'What Next? Some Questions to Think About'. *Scripting Power: Jana Sanskriti On and Offstage*, Ed. Dia Da Costa. Kolkata: Camp, pp. 174–183.

For Product Safety Concerns and Information please contact our EU representative GPSR@taylorandfrancis.com
Taylor & Francis Verlag GmbH, Kaufingerstraße 24, 80331 München, Germany

www.ingramcontent.com/pod-product-compliance
Lightning Source LLC
Chambersburg PA
CBHW051746230426
43670CB00012B/2189